Born to Overcome

†

Linda Robinson

To Paul

With every blessing for now and the future.

Linda

2QT Limited (Publishing)

This First Edition published 2011 by
2QT Limited (Publishing)
Dalton Lane, Burton In Kendal
Cumbria LA6 1NJ
www.2qt.co.uk

Cover Design by Hilary Pitt
Cover Images supplied by Shutterstock.com

Printed in Great Britain
Lightening Source UK Ltd

A CIP catalogue record for this book is available
from the British Library
ISBN 978-1-908098-30-6

My Personal Thanks

Some time ago whilst in church, a lady said the Lord had given her a word for me. It came from the book of Ephesians Chapter one: *'To the praise of His glory'*.

I therefore thank the Lord for making this book possible and may it be 'to the praise of His Glory'.

In addition, many others have contributed to it becoming a reality, God knows who they are and so do they. A huge 'Thank you' also.

However, there are certain people who I must mention by name and they are:

Michael my husband, who is quite simply "The Best". Without his love, self-sacrifice, encouragement, support and great wisdom, I would never have completed what for me has been a mammoth task.

Irene Stalker whom God used to get this book started- Thank you for being such a huge encouragement and a steadfast and faithful friend who has stuck closer than a brother.

Mary Fisher, my mentor and spiritual Mother. Your prayers and love have upheld me in the tough times of character shaping!

Johnette Irving, whom the Lord has used as a facilitator of so many of His exploits. Thank you my friend. I truly appreciate you.

The Christoffersen Family for showing me what it is like to be an 'adopted' daughter of the God of Heaven. I love you all so very much.

Finally, a huge thank you to Fran Parkinson, my co-worker and Editor in Chief! God truly performed a miracle when he brought you alongside me Fran and I thank Him for you!

Preface

We are, to quote the song: "An army of ordinary people." It is the Commander of this army and He alone that is extraordinary and today He, the Lord Jesus Christ is saying to this army of ordinary people that there has to be a shift, from us allowing circumstances, our perceived inadequacies and others, to hinder the way we walk out our Christian faith, to a steadfast focus on Him.

Whereas these aforementioned influences bring us into limitation, today is the season of liberation. Jesus is saying to His church that for what is coming it is imperative to realise that He really must be the centre and main focus of our lives. He is saying, that for his people to do the mighty exploits mentioned in the book of Daniel, ('...but the people who know their God will be strong and carry out great exploits' Daniel 11:32) we do need to know our God at a deeper level because there will be forces at work attempting to thwart us from attaining what God has purposed for His church in the latter days.

There is a vital necessity for the Disciples of Jesus Christ to rise up and to be "Overcomers" in these increasingly challenging days. I write this book as an ordinary member of the Body, in the hope that it may be source of encouragement to those of us who are pursuing to know Jesus more. It is written for those who are not content with mediocrity but whose desire is to live lives totally sold out for Him whilst at the same time hungering after a visible extension of His Kingdom in the areas in which He has placed us.

It is hoped that by the end of this book, a greater understanding will have been acquired regarding:

1. The power and authority we possess as sons and daughters of the God of Heaven and Earth and co-heirs with the King of Kings.

2. The assurance we truly have - that victory is ours in Christ Jesus alone and not from our own strength and resources, and finally:

3. How we can be those, who increasingly overcome and appropriate victory into our own lives and the lives of others, in these ever increasing dark days.

My heart-felt desire is that when ordinary, nameless Christians like myself, read these pages and share some of the many experiences of struggles and victories I have had, the Holy Spirit will come and impart his encouragement, love, power and enabling as only He can.

Chapter One

There will be trouble ahead

My dear friends, we are living in an age both inside the church and out, where discipline and obedience to authority are not the "in-Words". To God, however, and to those who wish to be Overcomers in Him, these words and their acceptance of them are vital in view of what lies before the Church of Jesus Christ.

At the beginning of 2011, I read the following extract from a compilation of writings produced in 1911, under the heading of "The Overcomer" and entitled:

'1911 A NEW ERA
'With justice He judges and makes war...' Rev 19 v 11

> The Book of Revelation is a book of war, and strikingly corresponds to the Book of Joshua with its history of war on earth, led by an invisible but real Captain, who is revealed to the visible leader on the eve of his first great battle on the Canaan side of Jordan river. Joshua was the visible leader, but he acted under the direct command of the Lord Himself, and the war never ceased until the

whole land was subdued by the hosts of the Lord. In the wilderness the people were a murmuring self-centred crowd occupied with their own troubles, but over Jordan it was "aggressive warfare" and peace was not to be thought of whilst an enemy remained to be destroyed.

Even so in the Apocalypse it is all war, but on a far vaster scale than in the small land of Canaan, for it depicts in panoramic style, great and terrible conflicts with great and terrible super-human powers arrayed against the God of Heaven, with the earth and the world of men as the battle ground, showing that the world is trending – not as men vainly hope, toward "universal peace" but - to universal war, in which the dominating factor will be great principalities and powers in the realm of the heavens, and when – by the time all reaches this great climax - the translated saints will be with the Lord on the Throne, sharing with Him the closing scenes of the Great War (bold mine) which began far back behind the story of Eden.

Dr. Pierson has pointed out that we are already well into this "War of the Ages"; but alas the greater number of the "Lord's army" are still unprepared and not even "over Jordan" but in the wilderness, occupied with their own personal needs, and not fighting... Nevertheless the light is breaking on many, and the Captain is awakening some of His sleeping soldiers by the cry of their fellows, "The Philistines are upon thee, O Samson;" whilst not a few who have longed to hold to the peace days of the rapidly fading past, are forced into the fighting line by the attacks of the enemy, even whilst resenting the call, rung out by the watchers on the watch-tower, discerning the gathering armies of the foe.

How the light is breaking may be seen in one extract from a letter written by a worker in India to a veteran missionary there, in which the writer says, "It almost appears to me we are on the threshold of a NEW ERA, if what is taught in the OVERCOMER was really put into practice by the church. If God is giving us new light on so important a subject it must be for a definite purpose. Maybe what is indicated in Matthew 7 v 22, as a state of deception into which a part of the church will fall, will now very soon take definite shape. We shall see mighty miracles worked in the church in the Name of our Lord, but energised by spirits not subject to Him...." We are convinced with the writer of this letter that we are on the eve of a "new era" if the church awakens to see the War with the powers of evil, and how she may triumph by the power of God.

To this end we must go forward into 1911 prepared for war with the enemy, and put aside all hope of peace in the church until it is based on righteousness. We are only just beginning to realise that there is a making for peace which arouses war, and a "war" which makes for "peace". We ourselves have yielded ground for "peace" sake which we have afterwards found to be surrender of ground to the adversary working to gain his ends under a flag of "peace". Now we see that the peace of God is based on righteousness, and the peace of the enemy's making covers up unrighteousness.

Therefore all things today must be tested at the foundation, and where there is a wonderful experience alongside of a dullness of vision to see the right and wrong of action, we must doubt the source of peace until all else is brought to the plummet of righteousness. The One on the white horse "made war" in "righteousness" and righteousness must be the breastplate of our armour in the coming year.'

Author Unknown

As I read the above article, which was written a hundred years ago, I realised that three years later, the world was plunged into a time of great darkness and tumult with the onset of the First World War. This war, just like the previous writer described the war in the Book of Revelation, was called 'The Great War'. It was centred on Europe, began in the summer of 1914 and ended in November 1918. Interestingly, this conflict involved all of the world's great powers assembled in two opposing alliances.

Shortly after reading this article, I found some CD's that had been issued for free by the Sunday Telegraph newspaper; they too were about the First World War. They were entitled, *The Century of Warfare - Part One: Countdown to Armageddon*. And the description of the contents in brief said,

'*As the 20th Century dawned, Europe was enjoying one of it's longest ever periods of peace and prosperity. But forces were at work which would soon bring unprecedented death and destruction.*'

Then in Part Two: A revolution In Warfare, it read,

'*1914-18 saw the introduction of weapons which transformed the way in which future wars would be fought...*'

Does anything sound familiar here?

As I pondered on all that I had read, I then considered the situation we find ourselves in at the beginning of 2011.

Could it be possible that we, too, are on the brink of 'A NEW ERA'? The number 11, in biblical numerology, is the number of Transition, with number 12 being the number of Governmental Authority. As one surveys the increasingly decadent and corrupt socio-economic climate, the damage being done to our environment, the ever increasing world-wide conflicts of peoples of every nation, tribe and tongue, the natural disasters, the growth of radical Islam and the intensifying hatred of Israel and things Jewish and the Christian church, we could also be forgiven for thinking that we are on the brink of a new era: this new era being the final countdown to the ushering in of Jesus the Messiah for His promised second coming. The new weapons mentioned in the Sunday Telegraph CD were the machine gun, the tank, the fighter, the bomber, the submarine and the aircraft carrier. Yet we are told as Christians that the weapons of our warfare are not carnal, but mighty IN GOD. When I look at the words "mighty in God" I realise that in order to fight, survive and prevail in these days of battle against the world, the flesh and the devil, we have to be immersed, covered and entrenched in God.

For too long, the Church has been rendered ineffective and unable to take her rightful stand in the world because of the inability of many of the individuals within it, to realise that we are in a war, and this war began the day we said, "yes" to Jesus and, "no" to sin, the world and the devil. For too long we have been 'passive' and 'defensive' instead of being 'active' and 'aggressive' in our fight against our enemies.

Of course, we have to remember who our foe is, and scripture makes it quite clear in Ephesians 6:12,

'For our struggle is not against flesh and blood, but against the rulers, against the authorities, against the powers of this dark world and against the spiritual forces of evil in the heavenly realms.'

This war is totally different to the types of war fought on earth as 2 Corinthians 10:3-4 explains,

'For though we live in the world, we do not wage war as the world does. The weapons we fight with are not the weapons of the world. On the contrary, they have divine power to demolish strongholds. We demolish arguments and every pretension that sets itself up against the knowledge of God, and we take captive every thought to make it obedient to Christ.'

A time for intimacy

Over and over again in scripture, we read about our brethren; for example, Habakkuk who, like many of us, was terribly despondent about the state of his surrounding environment. He was living in days similar to our own; days of trouble, violence, iniquity, perverse judgements, superseding righteous ones, and he constantly cried out to God in complaint. Reading the first couple of chapters of Habakkuk, reveal the extent of the prophet's distress but then from Chapter 3, we witness a turnaround in his demeanour as Habakkuk goes into the Lord's presence and begins to worship and ponder upon the greatness of God; so much so that by the end of the book, a complete transformation has taken place, and we see that he is so enraptured with His Lord that he appears oblivious to his circumstances and intent only on worshipping.

The reason for this is because when we go into the presence of the Lord, we are strengthened as God reveals more of Himself; His faithfulness, love, power, holiness, majesty and might. The more time we spend with God, the mightier He becomes and the smaller our problems become. We begin to see things through the eyes of faith with a godly perspective. Our God is on the throne! He is not defeated but victorious! If we are walking in obedience to Him we can truly rest in the knowledge that He is watching over us as we come and go, both now and forever. (See Psalm 121:8. NLT)

Although it may seem bizarre for some of us to think that despite the troubled times we are in, we hear time and time again the prophets of God saying to us,

'The time of singing has come...' that, *'we are in the season of the Bride and the Bridegroom.'*

It is in this place of His presence that intimacy is discovered and strength to overcome is found. He is all we need and the day for that to move from being mere head knowledge to true heart knowledge has dawned.

A further example of this truth is found as we look at the Psalms that King David wrote, and consider the amount of persecution and opposition he had to endure in his lifetime. We see before us a man who was constantly to be found in the Lord's presence and it was there that time and time again he found the strength to overcome and continue towards his God-given destiny. Sadly, this is not the strategy employed by the Church at large; it can't be because, if it were, many of us would find ourselves in a different place from where we are at present.

We would be more passionate for Christ, more willing to be witnesses, we would not give up so easily when obstacles appear but press on, trusting in God and seeking Him for our breakthrough, and we would be filled with more power.

The good news is, however, that God has not given up on us, and the opportunity to forget all that is behind and now to lay hold of that for which Christ has laid hold of us is still available. As we read the following verses from the Psalms, let us be encouraged and make that decision to spend more time in His presence,

'You will show me the path of life; In your presence is fullness of joy; At your right hand are pleasures evermore.' (Psalm 16:11)

'Hear my cry, O God, Attend to my prayer. From the end of the earth I will cry to you, when my heart is overwhelmed; Lead me to the rock that is higher than I. For you have been a shelter for me, A strong tower from the enemy. I will abide in your tabernacle forever; I will trust in the shelter of your wings.' (Psalm 61:1-4)

'My soul, wait silently for God alone, For my expectation is from Him. He only is my rock and my salvation; He is my defence; I shall not be moved. In God is my salvation and my glory; The rock of my strength, And my refuge is in God. Trust in Him at all times, you people; Pour out your heart before Him; God is a refuge for us.' (Psalm 62:5-8)

I personally believe that this new era into which we are entering, will be the likes of something never experienced before, and unless we are soaked in the love and power of Jesus, we will be unable to face what is ahead, in the way God would have us do so i.e. from a position of victory. We can do this because Jesus won the victory on the cross at Calvary but He never said we would not have to take part in the struggle to appropriate this victory on earth. Indeed, scripture tells us how the enemy, knowing his time is short, will unleash demonic forces upon the earth which, for a time, will seemingly prevail against God's people. (See Daniel 7:21-22 as just one example.)

This is the day of right and total alignment, not only to the plans and purposes of God, but to God himself. This is the day for intimacy with our Commander in Chief. Knowing Him will cause us to love Him and trust Him, and move us into faith and security from fear, for whatever lies before us as the church of Jesus Christ. Furthermore, we are instructed as children of God to understand the times and seasons we are in, and like the sons of "Issachar" be able to discern the signs. Intimacy with God will bring us into that place:

'Surely the Lord God does nothing, unless He reveals His secret to His servants the prophets.' (Amos 3:7)

The final countdown

In Matthew 24:3-13, Jesus is talking to His disciples about the Signs of the Times and the End of the Age,

> 'As Jesus was sitting on the Mount of Olives, the disciples came to him privately. "Tell us," they said, "when will this happen, and what will be the sign of your coming and of the end of the age?" Jesus answered: "Watch out that no-one deceives you. For many will come in my name, claiming, I am the Christ, and will deceive many. You will hear of wars and rumours of wars but see to it that you are not alarmed. Such things must happen, but the end is still to come. Nation will rise against nation, and kingdom against kingdom. There will be famines and earthquakes in various places. All these are the beginnings of birth pains. Then you will be handed over to be persecuted and put to death, and you will be hated by all nations because of me. At that time many will turn away from the faith and will betray and hate each other, and many false prophets will appear and deceive many people. Because of the increase of wickedness the love of most will grow cold, but he who stands firm to the end will be saved."'

Everything found in the above verses is already a reality on earth. Notice it says that we are not to be alarmed, and that famines and earthquakes and wars are the beginnings of birth pains. Anyone who has given birth knows that the birth pains start to grow in intensity and the space between the pains forever gains momentum until it culminates with the birth of the child. I am confident, that if we were to analyse the number of recurring earthquakes as just one example of how the "labour" for Christ's coming has progressed, we would notice that they are happening more often than they were, say ten years ago. Even in Cumbria, we felt the impact of two earthquakes in less than a month at the end of 2010 and the beginning of 2011.

If the world is even aware that something is not right, how much more should we sit up, take notice and ensure that we are prepared for the greatest battle which has already started, is intensifying, and will ultimately result in Victory for the Body Of Christ; but NOT without a FIGHT!

There is a strong warning in these verses, namely that the love of most will grow cold and that we are going to have to endure persecutions, sometimes death and hardships, the like of which have never been experienced before. The words of Matthew Chapter 24 could fill us with trepidation, dread and hopelessness, but Jesus says to the Disciples, 'See to it that you are not alarmed!' In other words, He is telling them to take the initiative to ensure that they do not become so paralysed by fear of their circumstances that they plummet into the abyss of despair and unbelief. If He is telling them this then it must be possible, that even in the midst of unimaginable distress, in Christ, we are able to stand firm to the end and be saved.

I believe that the purpose of this book is part of the equipping to attain that end. It is time to realise and understand who we are as God's children, and that we need to be those who stand firm because we are born to overcome!

Chapter Two

"Who are you?"

Before we can live lives as Overcomers we need to have a deeper understanding of the truths hidden in God's Word regarding who we are in Christ. The whole of this book could be spent dwelling on this topic alone, but this is not its purpose. Instead, my aim is to highlight the necessity of knowing who we are and give a few pointers on the subject.

The fact is that the church now, more than ever, requires a fresh revelation of our true standing in Christ and the potential that lies within us because of what Jesus did for us on the cross. This is the time, I believe, to shift from being a Body with potential, into a Body of manifestation. If we remain at potential level then the world around us and we, ourselves, remain mostly unchanged.

However, for this shift to take place, we need to know who we are, so that great courage and risk-taking faith can rise up within us, as it did with Joshua and Caleb in the story of Numbers 13. It is here that God spoke to Moses and instructed him to send spies into the Land of Canaan, which was the land He had promised to give to the Israelites.

You probably know the story, but at the end of the mission, only two people were prepared to be obedient to God's call to take possession of the land. Most of the Israelites were

17

petrified and overcome with fear because of the giants they had seen, and saw themselves as grasshoppers, rather than their true identity as Children of God.

We need to cry out to God for a breakthrough in the knowledge of who we really are in Christ; what can be achieved in us through Christ; and attained outwardly by the manifestation of Christ. When this happens, we truly will see ourselves, and the world, with all its challenges, in a different light. For example, if all Christians truly believed in the truth, '*I can do all things through Christ who strengthens me.*' (Philippians 4:13) then planet earth would be a different place.

So many of us, including myself, look at what God calls us to and feel extremely uncomfortable and exceedingly stretched, because it goes beyond our own limitations. However, we need to grasp and hold on to the truth that when God calls, God equips. I have recently received three pieces of download from the Lord which apply to my latest sermon title, based on Moses and the burning bush; when God appoints, God anoints and He never disappoints! In fact, often, if one is involved in something that can be achieved quite easily through human effort alone, then there is a possibility that it is a good idea as opposed to a God idea.

Calling brings opposition

In spite of the call to write this book, defeat and discouragement have looked me in the eye on numerous occasions, from varying sources and situations. In fact, there have been times when I have even felt very close to giving up with this work, because of the relentless pressures and challenges. One of the major obstacles has been finding the time, in what, for most of us is a busy life, and then there has been a tangible inner struggle to sit and trust God to download what to write.

However, despite the negative voices telling me what a waste of time this is - which I am sure you can relate to in some form or other - and despite the difficulties, I made a decision not to quit. Instead, I decided to stand on the word which says that no matter what comes against us,

'He who is in you is greater than he who is in the world..' (1 John 4:4) and in and through Him, we can have ultimate victory over sin, the world, the devil and self. This is something we all need to remember, believe and act upon because if we don't, we will instead BE OVERCOME by the ever increasing darkness.

As I look around and see the battering, simply accepted by so many of God's people as being part of life, righteous anger rises up. I know that just because we are Christians we cannot expect to live a trouble-free existence but, because of our identity in Christ, WE CAN expect to be Overcomers in every situation. That is why it has been important to persevere with this project; during my relatively short life as a Christian (18 years), God has proven beyond every conceivable doubt that He is faithful in every situation. The deliverance process has not been instantaneous, and indeed some afflictions or problems are still in process, but past experience of God's total faithfulness in my own life has shifted enormously the level of doubt to faith.

In terms of the Christian Walk, this does not also mean that total victory has been won in every area of life. However God makes the promise to all who walk in obedience that He will perfect that which concerns us. Notice how we are not the initiators of this - God is! Yes, there will still be struggles with sin at times; not everyone who is prayed for will receive healing; not every problem prayed about will be resolved in the way imagined, or even at the speed we would like. However, yielding to God, trusting in Him, His faithfulness and the truth of His word which says that the Kingdom is advancing, we are called to,

'.... *press on, that I may lay hold of that for which Christ Jesus has also laid hold of me. Brethren, I do not count myself to have apprehended; but one thing I do, forgetting those things which are behind and reaching forward to those things which are ahead, I press toward the goal for the prize of the upward call of God in Christ Jesus.'* (Philippians 3:12-14)

In salvation is found the ability to overcome

Another key to realising our true identity as Overcomers in Christ, is revelation and understanding of the term "Salvation." Many Christians I have questioned and heard speak on salvation, rarely ever speak of it meaning anything else apart from being "saved" from hell, and being able to look forward to eternal life. Although these two facts are wonderful in themselves, I now wish to explain the meaning of "salvation" as revealed by the Lord to myself several years ago. I was reading Ephesians, where Paul is praying for the believers to receive spiritual wisdom,

'Therefore, I also, after I heard of your faith in the Lord Jesus and your love for all the saints, do not cease to give thanks, making mention of you in my prayers: that the God of our Lord Jesus Christ, the Father of glory, may give to you the spirit of wisdom and revelation in the knowledge of Him, the eyes of your understanding being enlightened; that you may know what is the hope of his calling, what are the riches of the glory of His inheritance in the saints.' (Ephesians 1:15-18)

As I began to meditate on these verses in the New King James version of the 'Spirit Filled Life Bible', I felt led to see how it explained the true meaning of wisdom. The word has two meanings in the Greek and the one applicable to this scripture is "sophia" which means: comprehensive insight; Christian enlightenment; a right application of knowledge; or, and this was the meaning that grabbed me, 'insight into the true nature of things.' I firmly believe that the Holy Spirit was revealing something of vital importance so I then looked up "salvation", "soteria" and was delighted to read that it not only means salvation from a lost eternity, but also; deliverance, preservation, soundness, prosperity, happiness, rescue and general well-being. It went on to say, *Salvation is a present possession with an ever increasing fuller realisation in the future.'*

As I delved further into this subject of what salvation actually should mean to Christians, my faith levels began to soar. I read that, *'In Christ's suffering and death, he bore more than our sins. The penalty for sin is death, but Christ did not need to suffer as he did to provide for our atonement.'*

Chapter 53 of Isaiah tells us why He suffered, *'He suffered to bear our grief's and sorrows'* (v 4) and *'He suffered for our peace and healing'* [1] (v5). As I realised the impact of those words, I began to weep in thankfulness for what God has done for me, it changed my life. Is it any wonder that the scriptures say that the feet carrying this message are beautiful! (See Isaiah 52:7 and Romans 10:15)

It is far more profound than I had ever realised when I first came to faith, and I am still working it out with fear and trembling. As we walk closer with the Lord, I am absolutely convinced that the meaning of salvation is appropriated within us to an ever increasing degree, if we will make it our goal to pursue it.

---

1 Spirit Filled life Bible page: 1032 Kingdom Dynamics

We are a Kingdom people

Our identity as joint-heirs with Christ means that we are called to be His witnesses of the transforming power and truth of the Gospel. This Gospel we are to be witnesses of, is not just a Gospel of Salvation, but a Gospel of the Kingdom. We are called to be 'Kingdom people', with a Kingdom mentality, who no longer view the world from an earthly position but from a Kingdom perspective. Jesus had a great deal to say about the Kingdom.

A very poignant statement He made in my view, is the verse in Matthew 11:12, *'And from the days of John the Baptist until now, the kingdom suffers violence, and the violent take it by force.'*

We must begin to get this fact into our spirits, believe it and act upon it, because it is true.

In the "Kingdom Dynamics" section of the 'NKJ Spirit-filled' Bible it says this,

> 'Conflict and the Kingdom: Jesus asserts the violence of the kingdom. The unique grammatical construction of the text does not make clear if the kingdom of God is the victim of violence or if, as the kingdom advances in victory, it does so through violent spiritual conflict and warfare. But the context does. Jesus' references to the non-religious style of John and the confrontational, miraculous ministry of Elijah, teach that the Kingdom of God makes its penetration by a kind of violent entry opposing the human status quo. It transcends the "softness" of staid religious formalism (11:8) and exceeds the pretension of child's play (vv 16, 17). It refuses to "dance to the music" of society's expectation that the religious community provide either entertainment ("we played the flute") or dead traditionalism ("we mourned"). Jesus defines

the "violence of His kingdom's expansion by defining the "sword" and the "fire" He has brought as different from the battle techniques of political or military warfare (compare Matthew 10:34-39 and Luke 12:49-53 with John 18:36). The upheaval caused by the Kingdom of God is not caused by political provocation or armed advance. It is the result of God's order shaking relationships, households, cities, and nations by the entry of the Holy Spirit's power working in people.'

The successful advancement of the Kingdom is therefore totally dependent on God, however, He has decided to achieve this by manifesting His power in and through us, His people. We have a choice whether or not to participate. If we allow God to use us, then we are going to have to learn to believe and trust Him with our lives.

This will involve stepping out of our comfort zones and exercising our faith. As I said earlier, calling brings with it opposition, and this means that we will suffer tribulation as the opposing forces of darkness stand against us. Christians who live trouble-free lives are not involved in the Gospel of the Kingdom and the person who said, 'The greater the call, the bigger the devil' definitely knew what they were talking about.

Yes, we can rest assured that as we walk forward in the spirit of an Overcomer, the arrows are going to fly and we will receive wounds, but this should not stop or hinder us permanently. We are called to press into the one who is our refuge and fortress and press on as did Jesus and other mighty men and women of God in the Bible. David did not give up. Joseph pursued his dream. Deborah won the battle!

It is time to learn from the examples of the past so that we are armed for the future. The word of God tells us that in the last days, times of tribulation are coming, the likes of which have never been seen before,

'for then there will be great tribulation, such as has not been since the beginning of the world until this time, no, nor ever shall be. And unless those days were shortened, no flesh would be saved; but for the elect's sake those days will be shortened.' (Matthew 24:21-22)

At the beginning of the 19th century, the Holy Spirit was prompting Christians to write about Overcoming; a hundred years on, how the message needs reinforcing. We are nearer the end than they were then and this is very evident by what is happening in the world.

It is time to recognise that Satan is an already defeated foe, that his authority was taken away by Jesus on the cross at Calvary, and that in Christ we truly are more than conquerors. 2 Corinthians 4:8 reminds us,

'We are hard-pressed on every side, but not crushed; perplexed, but not in despair; persecuted but not abandoned; struck down, but not destroyed.'

In my favourite bible, the NKJ Spirit-Filled Life version, there is a sub-heading just before this verse called, 'Cast down but unconquered!" In the NIV Application Bible, the sub-heading is different; here it says 'Treasures in jars of clay!'

Jars of clay with treasure within

Who are you? Who am I?

We are just jars of clay so to speak, BUT we have treasure in our jars, and that treasure is the awesome and insurmountable power of the Holy Spirit. This is the amazing legacy which Jesus left for us. The Holy Spirit, whose "dunamis" power raised Jesus from the dead, lives in God's people today, but we are failing to appropriate it. We have to stop looking at ourselves and look to the one dwelling in us! It is ALL about Him!

Our victory over every circumstance comes from Jesus, because of ourselves we can do nothing (see John 15:5, 'I am the vine; you are the branches. He who abides in Me and I in him, bears much fruit; for without me you can do nothing.') Why is this so?

2 Corinthians 4:7 reads, *'To show that this all-surpassing power is from God and not from us.'*

It is vital that we get a true revelation of what these words are actually saying, because when we do, it will change our perspective on what we think we are able to accomplish for the advancement of the Kingdom. It is saying that God has purposely chosen weak, inadequate humans to be mantled with His authoritative power and do amazing things. In Christ our identity changes. We become partakers of the *'divine nature'*. (See 2 Peter 1:4) and part of that nature is to be a warrior, overcoming every obstacle and gaining victory, no matter how many times we may stumble and fall on the way!

One of the clearest examples of this truth is found with Gideon in Judges Chapter 6. He was hiding from the enemy, threshing wheat in a wine-press in the hope that he would not be discovered. A member of the tribe of Manasseh, Gideon was the youngest son in his family but this is how the Angel of the Lord addressed him in verse 12,

'The Lord is with you, you mighty man of valour!'

Verse 14 says,

'Then the Angel of the Lord turned to him and said, "Go in this might of yours, and you shall save Israel from the hand of the Midianites. Have I not sent you?"'

The conversation continues,

'So he (Gideon) said to Him "O my Lord, how can I save Israel? Indeed my clan is the weakest in Manasseh, and I am the least in my Father's house." And the Lord said "Surely I will be with you, and

you shall defeat the Midianites as one man.'"

Those of you familiar with the story know that God delivered the Israelites from a much stronger enemy using Gideon as the deliverer. A further point of interest is how God reduced an initial army of 32,000 men down to just 300.

In Chapter 7:2 God explains to Gideon why he does not approve of Gideon initially amassing such a great army,

'And the Lord said to Gideon, "The people who are with you are too many for me to give the Midianites into their hands, lest Israel claim glory for itself against Me, saying My own hand has saved Me."'

The point I am making is that if God calls us to a task, no matter how impossible it may appear in the natural realm, we can do it in confidence because He equips us with His divine power and strength. In fact, if the job we are feeling called to do is well within our human capabilities, I would like to challenge you to dream bigger dreams! I know I have said this before but we need to hear it over and over again.

Our God is the God of the impossible and although it does not necessarily mean we are all called to fight a great war like Gideon, it will often mean that in our own strength alone, it will not be possible to get the job done.

We were born for success as well as suffering. (Consider the life of Jesus) We were born to establish Kingdom atmospheres wherever we go. We were born to be the head and not the tail. We carry within us the DNA of non-quitters. We were born to overcome! You can be an Overcomer whether you feel like it or not because the fact that you are one, is not based upon you as a person, but on your position in Christ.

Christ came to this earth to bring salvation and overcome the works of the enemy, and when He ascended into heaven, He delegated the task to us His people. He is the Name above all names.

'Far above all principality and power and might and dominion and every name that is named, not only in this age but also in that which is to come. And He put all things under His feet and gave Him to be head over all things to the church, which is His body, the fullness of Him who fills all in all.' (Ephesians 1:21-23)

Chapter Three

You are a person who is loved unconditionally

I have been a Christian for eighteen years and during that time I have read that Jesus loves me, I have been told by others that He loves me and I have always believed that He loves me. Recently however, I have begun to sense a deeper, heart-felt knowledge of this love and I know that partly the reason this has taken place, is because of His grace, my commitment to trust and live a life of obedience to Christ (see 1 John 5:3-4) and the tenacity in pursuing to know Him more.

You see, our God is a God of relationship and a relationship is a two-way thing. As I have grown, and continue to grow in the knowledge of Christ's love, God is showing me that Jesus is all we need to live as Overcomers in this world. (See 1 John 5:5). Some time ago, I was addressing a group of women and the Lord told me to tell them that living the life of an Overcomer does not necessarily mean that a bad situation changes but that our mind-set and attitude, in the midst of tribulation, remains positive and trusting.

As an example we can look at the account of Paul and Silas in prison, in Acts 16. They had been beaten up with rods and put into stocks and must have been in terrible pain. In spite of their traumatic situation however, the bible says that at midnight they were praying and singing hymns and that the prisoners were listening to them.

They were living in an "overcoming" mode despite their circumstances. How were they able to do that? I firmly believe that it is because of the love of Jesus in their lives. They loved Him so much that they were prepared to suffer and continue in service to Him. However, 1 John 4 v 19 says, *'We love Him because He first loved us.'*. Yes, they loved Jesus but only because they knew of His love for them.

I had planned a different title for this Chapter but the Holy Spirit spoke and said that unless we first of all have a revelation of God's love for us, then we will not get very far in our pursuit of living our lives as Overcomers. It is not just enough to seek the Lord earnestly or spend time in His presence in praise and worship; it will not suffice, even if we read and meditate regularly on the Word of God and if we walk in obedience; although all these things are very valuable in themselves.

We have to go beyond all these things and have a heart-felt, experiential assurance of the truth, that God delights in us and loves us unconditionally. We are His delight, we are the apple of His eye and our names are engraved in the palm of His hand.

If we have never had an in-depth experience of God's love then we will never have the faith to trust Him enough to live lives as Overcomers. 1 John 4 verse 18 says that, 'perfect love casts out fear'. If this is not true for us then we need to ask for the Lord to reveal His love to our hearts. It is not enough just knowing it, we have to feel it! We have to have experience of this truth.

Summer of romance

About ten years ago, I was an example of a child of God who had yet to begin to experience the love He had for me. At this time, I felt compelled to go to a certain Christian Camp being held down in Cornwall but when the theme for the conference arrived in the post, I recollect having felt quite disappointed. The whole week away was to be spent learning of God's love in Jesus. I remember thinking to myself that I knew that Jesus loved me, so why did I have to learn about it any further?

The first morning of the camp commenced with Communion, the time we as God's people remember the price that was paid for us on Calvary. As the bread and wine went around, the love of God which began to pour down on me was almost too much to bear. It was almost as if Jesus was saying to me personally that I was loved so much that I was worth dying for. I will never forget holding the goblet of wine and, for what seemed like ages, being unable to drink because of the tears that were pouring down my face. The shedding of Jesus' blood for me, became, in that instant a reality and I began the journey of discovering how wonderful and marvellous it is to know that I am unconditionally loved.

The second experience I feel I would like to share, is about the time I received an unexpected gift from a dear friend of mine. The book is entitled "Come Away with Me" written by Jonathan Hindsley and is based on a prophetic meditation on the Song of Solomon.

One evening, I was reading the book in conjunction with the Song of Solomon in the Bible, when the verses twelve and fourteen from chapter two stood out,

'The flowers appear on the earth; the time of singing has come, and the voice of the turtledove is heard in our land...'

'O my dove, in the clefts of the rock, in the secret places of the cliff, let me see your face, let me hear your voice; for your voice is sweet and your face is lovely.'

Once again God's presence became tangible in the room and I began to praise Him in tongues. As I was praising, the tongue changed and began to sound like a gentle cooing. I know this might sound strange to some readers but this is what happened and it was truly beautiful. I really felt like I was Jesus' dove and that he was speaking to me personally. A week later my family and I flew to the Island of Corfu on holiday and to my delight, all week I kept hearing the cooing of doves from the trees.

As time passes and my walk with the Lord becomes more intimate, I am grasping more and more what it is like to be loved unconditionally and it is revolutionising my life, especially in the area of "overcoming".

There is no condemnation in Christ!

It is time for the church to slam the door on the voice of the accuser, *'Forgetting what is behind'*. We're amateur psychologists these days trying to remember all our pasts; trying to reason why our mothers did this and our fathers did that; to explain all our idiosyncrasies and quirks.

The Bible doesn't deal with us in this way. It pronounces us sinners, tells us we are forgiven and loved and then says to get on with it, to look up and forward! All the great people of faith in Hebrews 11 looked forward. So did Jesus: he endured the cross *'for the joy set before him'*. (Hebrews 12:2)

Instead of allowing ourselves to dwell on the mistakes of the past we have to press forward and focus on laying hold of all that God has given us in Christ Jesus. Overcomers shed the baggage of the past and look up and press on forward.

The enemy will resort to anything to make us feel unloved, and another strategy is to thrust guilt upon us when we have sinned, and to incessantly whisper in our ears that we are neither good or worthy enough for God to love or use us. I have suffered this form of attack on numerous occasions and no doubt it will continue.

However, I no longer accept the devil's attacks passively and I do my utmost not to allow the enemy to beat me up with feelings of guilt when I make mistakes. I have already repented of the way I lived my life before Christ, on the day I accepted Him as Lord and Saviour and acknowledged my need for salvation and forgiveness of my sins. Unfortunately, the enemy sometimes needs reminding of this fact because he often tries to burden people with the past when the past has been forgiven.

When I make mistakes, I repent and move on, fully aware that as a mere human, I will suffer set-backs and it is all part of the learning process of becoming a disciple.

That is what we all need to do. Take as an example, the words of Saint Paul who writes in Philippians 3:12-14,

'Not that I have already attained or am already perfected; but I press on to lay hold of that for which Christ Jesus has also laid hold of me. Brethren, I do not count myself to have apprehended; but one thing I do, forgetting those things which are behind and reaching forward to those things that are ahead, I press toward the goal for the prize of the upward call of God in Christ Jesus.'

If the enemy sidles up to me now, I remind him of God's Word - in other words I wield the sword of the Spirit. (See Ephesians 6:17)

To wield the sword of the spirit, is to speak out (preferably aloud), the truth of God's words as an antidote to the lies of the devil. For example, if one has had a bad day whereby the fruit of the Spirit: i.e. patience, long suffering etc. has been seemingly in limited supply, the way to overcome is firstly, to accept that we have sinned and pray for more grace and enabling from God in the area of our weaknesses.

Secondly, we repent and ask forgiveness both of the Lord and if possible also the person we have wronged. If however despite doing that, the feelings of guilt linger and we still hear little voices telling us that we are no good and so on, then we have to begin to speak out the truth of God's word. In this case, a good scripture would be 1 John 1:9,

'If we confess our sins, he is faithful and just and will forgive us our sins and purify us from all unrighteousness.'

This strategy cannot fail if we will but persevere, (See James 4:7, which tells us to *'resist the devil and he will flee'*) although on occasion it can take time for the position of victory to be appropriated which in the above mentioned case, would be that these negative thoughts disappear and peace is restored to our spirits.

The bible tells us very clearly in John 8:44, that the devil is the Father of lies, whereas in Titus 1:2, Numbers 23:19 and Hebrews 6:18 it says that God cannot lie.

The question we have to ask ourselves is this: 'Who are we going to believe, God or the devil?'

I am saddened and astounded at the sheer volume of Christians who choose to believe the lie instead of the truth despite the fact that God also says that His word is truth (See John 17:17, Psalm 19:7, Proverbs 30:5; as examples of this).

If we take the stance to believe God and accept that when He says His words are true, it is the truth, then we have to believe that the reason we are loved unconditionally is because God is love and demonstrated this by sending Jesus - irrespective of what we have or have not done. The truth is, that our being loved and accepted by Him, being valuable and precious to Him is not based on our actions but on what Jesus Christ accomplished for us in His death on the cross and in the resurrection.

In the NLT, 1 John 4:9-10 reads,

'God showed how much he loved us by sending his only son into the world so that we might have eternal life through him'.

This is real love- not that we loved God, but that he loved us and sent his Son as a sacrifice to take away our sins. This is indeed real love!

When we fail to believe God's Word to us, not only do we suffer defeat at the hands of the Father of Lies but are we not also saying that Christ's death on the cross was not sufficient? We need to approach this issue with honesty and where there is unbelief, cry out to God that He might help us to experience His love.

Receive His love

The following scriptures are a further indication of God's unconditional love for us. Read them, meditate on them, digest them, learn some of them off by heart, persevere with them, wield them, be blessed, encouraged and transformed by them, be restored by them, believe them and **OVERCOME BY THEM!**

Jeremiah 31:3:

'The Lord has appeared of old to me saying "Yes, I have loved you with an everlasting love. Therefore with loving kindness I have drawn you.'

Isaiah 43:4:

'Since you are precious and honoured in my sight and because I love you, I will give men in exchange for you.'

Ephesians 1:4-5:

'For He chose us in him before the creation of the world to be holy and blameless in His sight. In love He pre-destined us to be adopted as His sons through Jesus Christ in accordance with His pleasure and will.'

Song of Solomon 2:16:

'My beloved is mine and I am His.'

My final scripture also comes from the above book Chapter 2:4:

'He brought me to the banqueting house and his banner over me was love.'

Jesus came not only to be Lord and bring salvation for our souls, *'He came that we might have life to the full.'* (John 10:10). He died for us that we might live lives which overcome in any given situation.

We have been given the permission by God himself to go into the banqueting house of his provision and take what we need, when we need it, without fear, knowing with confidence that we are completely loved and accepted. I have already mentioned the scripture: 'Perfect love casts out fear.' (1 John 4:18) and that we need to have a true revelation of God's love for us before we can really begin to overcome in our lives.

We all know the scripture: John 3:16,

'For God so loved the world that he gave his only begotten son, that whoever believes in him should not perish but have everlasting life.'

The word "loved" in the above text is "agapao" and means unconditional love; love by choice and by act of the will. The word denotes unconquerable benevolence and un-defeatable goodwill. Agapao will never seek anything but the highest good for mankind. Agapao (the verb) and Agape (the noun) are the words for God's unconditional love. It does not need a chemistry, an affinity, or a feeling. Agapao is a word that exclusively belongs to the Christian community. It is a love virtually unknown to writers outside the New Testament.[2]

A revelation of this type of love is not always immediately acquired. It takes time and effort to develop our relationship with Jesus. Nevertheless, I firmly believe that these are the days when God wants us to press tenaciously into Him, so that we might know the height and depth of this un-surpassing love and become filled with the fullness of God. It is as we grow in the knowledge of his love that fullness will be realised and we will begin to walk as Overcomers in Christ.

2 NKJ Spirit-Filled Life Bible by Thomas Nelson Publishers, Nashville. Page 1578

Chapter Four

Oh yes we can by His grace!

Never having written a book before, it has to be said that this work is totally attributable to the wonderful grace of our Lord and Saviour Jesus Christ who says to us that, *'apart from Him we can do nothing'* (John 15:5), yet at the same time *'with God, nothing is impossible'* (Luke 1:37), and, *'we can do all things through Christ.'* (Philippians: 4:13).

I believe the book is for those like me who are not satisfied with 'visitations' of God's Holy Spirit, great though they are. No, this has been written to encourage those who are hungry and in pursuit of God and want His habitation and are prepared to go through whatever is necessary to get there. "Ouch!" Yes, the truth is that if we want this to be a realisation in our lives, then we are going to have to be prepared to come up against many forms of opposition and overcome in His strength, many attempts to take us off course. Despite the tough times however, (and there will be many!), God is allowing these difficulties to strengthen us, put iron in our souls and make us more like Christ.

The enemy, who is petrified of those who really know their God and know who they are in Christ, will undoubtedly attempt to throw spanner after spanner into the works that God is doing in and through you. However, he will be defeated if we, despite the pain, sufferings and frustrations, keep our eyes on Jesus, remain steadfast in righteousness keeping our hearts right at all times and allow Him who is the author and finisher of our faith to lead us. (See Hebrews 12:2)

Prepared!

A good biblical example of this is found in the Book of Joshua which we have already visited. The generation of Israelites that had refused to believe God and do what He had called them to, had all died apart from Joshua and Caleb.

This next generation had been wandering in the wilderness and it is in this place that God prepared them for their destiny- for what lay ahead. It was here in a mundane backwater where nothing ever much happened, that He fed them, watered them and revealed to them his faithfulness, so that they knew that they could trust Him and believe in Him.

Then came the day when they were shaped and moulded and ready for the next season God had prepared. In Chapter 1 verse 2, we read how first of all Joshua received the command from God to arise and to enter into the land God had promised. Then in verse 10 it says that the people were told to make provision for themselves. You see, the time of having it all on a plate was over. God had given them everything over these past 40 years; it was almost as if they had been spoon-fed, but now it was time for them to step out in faith and be responsible for their own welfare.

In the Church, we have been living in a season where we have had every tool imaginable given to us, in order to be strong, mature Christians. Despite this, many are still not mature in faith and continue to be unprepared for what lies ahead, and the reason I believe is twofold. Firstly, an unwillingness to walk in uncompromising obedience and secondly, because tools are of no value, unless we use them and keep them in good condition.

Jesus is the Word, but how many of us spend sufficient time reading and heeding it. Praise and worship brings us into the presence of God, into the throne-room where we meet in fellowship and grow in love and knowledge of God whilst at the same time, receive His transforming power. Then there has been the ministry made available to heal, bring deliverance and challenge us to walk in the light.

What more can God do for us that He has not already done? If we have been Christians for years and we are not yet mature, it is no-one's fault but our own and it is time to consider our life-style choices and put the Lord in His rightful place, to enable us to reach our rightful place.

Notice how in Joshua Chapter 5 when the people had crossed over and had just arrived in the Promised Land, prior to embarking on what must have seemed an enormous challenge, God called the males to circumcision and then told them that the reproach of Egypt had been rolled back. In other words the past was gone - A new day had dawned, they were no longer slaves to sin but ready and prepared to go to a new level in God - He was now able to trust them with the calling to take the Land.

The Passing over

In Joshua Chapter 5 verse 10, the people then celebrated Passover. Passover was a timely reminder before the battle really commenced, that their success, as it was after the first Passover, was going to be totally attributable to God. In the New Testament we see that Jesus ate of the Passover before also facing His biggest challenge. But notice how at this celebration, Jesus says of the bread they are eating that it is His body and of the wine they were drinking, that it is His blood:

'And as they were eating, Jesus took bread, blessed and broke it, and gave it to the disciples and said, "Take, eat; this is my body." Then he took the cup and gave thanks and gave it to them, saying "Drink from it, all of you. For this is my blood of the new covenant"....' (Matthew 26:26-28).

Bearing this in mind (about the bread and the blood being Jesus' body and blood), let us revisit the Old Testament, where in Exodus Chapter 12 there were some regulations regarding whether or not one could be part of the Passover.

It says this in verse 45: *'A sojourner (temporary resident) and a hired servant shall not eat it'.*

As I pondered on these words, I wanted to share with you what I felt was being revealed. Unless we are truly committed to God, feeding regularly on Him and receiving the continual nourishment that comes from the Word (remember in John's Gospel, Jesus said He was the bread of life) we will be weak. Unless we are being constantly filled by the Holy Spirit and allow Him to reveal the power of Jesus' shed blood, in which is found life in abundance, we will be weak. Harsh though it may seem, the truth remains that if we do not do the above, we will never be in the correct position to receive what God has for us.

We might be saved but God has so much more for us to enter into before we leave earth and if we do not do this then we will not receive the rewards He wants to give us when we join Him.

Purpose and perspective

It is time for us to awake and arise! These words are expressing a need for commitment and commitment to God by His people at this time and it is just as important today as it was then. Why? Because just as they faced many huge challenges and did not receive the Promised Land handed on a plate, neither can we expect to do so. What we can expect however is that God by his grace, seeing that we do our part will do His. Joshua 18 verse 2-3 says this and serves as a stark warning,

'But there remained among the tribes of Israel seven tribes which had not yet received their inheritance.'

Then Joshua said to the children Israel, *'How long will you neglect to go and possess the land which the Lord your of your fathers has given you?'*

We can no longer afford to be those that neglect to possess what God has given us for the taking, not in our own personal Christian development, nor in extending the Kingdom. You see, God's children are purposed for a destiny, and that destiny is to exhibit to the earth the character and likeness of Jesus and advance the kingdom. Just as Jesus was a witness to the character of the Father, we are to be those same witnesses for Jesus and it is the same with the extension of His Kingdom. Wherever Jesus went, the Kingdom was made visible and we are expected to do the same.

The world does not need meetings, programmes and initiatives - it needs to see Jesus who is fairest of the fair, loveliest of the lovely, kindest of the kind, the most forgiving, the most wise, the most holy and the most powerful to name just a few of His attributes! If we want to exhibit these same qualities to the extent that they impact those around us and the Kingdom is seen on earth as it is in heaven, then we are going to have to firstly realise and understand that He is the one to do it, in and through us.

Furthermore, we need to be willing to accept, that in order for God to make us fit to be a sanctuary where He can dwell. We are going to have to allow Him to mould, discipline, shape us and bring about a total shift in our mind-set i.e. to view things from a heavenly perspective and to walk by faith and not by sight, to be those who call into being the things yet unseen as though they were, with belief in our hearts. In order for that to take place we are going to have to learn to trust Him like never before.

This is not easy; it took the Israelites 40 years of wanderings before they were ready; but one key to trusting Him is to know Him and a key to knowing Him is to walk righteously before Him. The Bible says,

'Who may worship in your sanctuary, Lord? Who may enter your presence on your holy hill? Those who lead blameless lives and do what is right, speaking the truth from sincere hearts. Those who refuse to gossip or harm their neighbours or speak evil of their friends. Those who despise flagrant sinners, and honor the faithful, and keep their promises even when it hurts. Those who lend money without charging interest, and who cannot be bribed to lie about the innocent. Such people will stand firm forever.' (NLT Psalm 15:1-5)

'The Lord is a friend to those who fear him. He teaches them his covenant.' (NLT Psalm 25: verses 12- 14).

Be thou my vision

My personal prayer over the last year or so has been the words of an old Hymn, 'Be THOU my vision, Lord of my Heart. NOUGHT be all else to me save that THOU ART.'

These are very powerful words and, believe you me, they are not to be prayed lightly. In my case, a few months after praying them, I found myself in a pit of absolute despair. I was in the prayer closet pouring my heart out to God and complaining of the unfairness and injustice of my situation, when the Lord brought to my heart these very same words. I could almost hear Him tangibly speaking and He said, how else could He ever be my vision, how else could I ever reach the place where, when the chips were down and there was no-one there for me, I would still be okay because of the deep awareness that He would always be there for me, no matter what.

I then realised that in order for Him to answer this prayer of mine, regardless of the fact that I walked in righteousness, (consider Joseph, falsely accused by Potiphar's wife and thrown into a cell for three years.) He was going to have to bring me into situations that were not going to be pleasant or easy until I reached the place where I really felt that knowing He was with me, was sufficient for my peace and comfort.

This is the hard truth we all have to face. It is easy to say that we want God but we have to ask ourselves the question do we really? True Christianity is definitely not for the faint-hearted! Scripture shows us that God leads His children through suffering before He brings them through to reach his glory.

'The Spirit Himself bears witness with our spirit that we are children of God and joint heirs with Christ, if indeed we suffer with Him, that we may also be glorified together' (Romans 8:17).

So many Christians fail to move from having potential to manifesting power, because they are not prepared to seek God for the ability and strength to overcome the challenges that are to be viewed as an integral part of our Walk. It is very rare to hear messages about suffering, sacrifice and self-denial preached in pulpits. Could the reason for this be attributed to the fact that these words do not feature in the vocabulary of many of those professing the Christian faith?

We have to be prepared to accept that without the cross there was and is no crown, and without pain there will be no gain. Jesus Christ's life exhibited these things and if we want to be joint heirs with him we have to lay down our lives and accept these things also, knowing however that we do not walk alone but that His grace is sufficient for every situation and circumstance no matter who you are or what you have done.

Psalm 23

We have established that the Lord first and foremost wants us to know that He loves us, He accepts us and that He will never leave but always be willing to lead us. A popular piece of scripture which wonderfully portrays the journey of grace to becoming an Overcomer is Psalm 23, *'The Lord is my Shepherd; I shall not want.'*

Notice how personal it is - David could have written 'our shepherd' but he was inspired by the spirit of God to write 'my shepherd' because the Lord desires to be a personal and relational God to His children. Notice how the first subject of focus is God and who He is - the one who protects, nurtures and comes alongside.

As we sit with Him these characteristics of His nature will become increasingly real for us and then with confidence we will be able to say, *'I shall not want.'*

How I long for the day when I can declare these words with total confidence! I know they are true with my head and there are so many other verses of scripture where God tells us that we will lack nothing if we walk in covenant with Him but there is still a work of grace in progress in terms of getting them into my heart and I am sure the same will apply to many of you reading this book too.

The second verse begins again with the focus on God. Notice that it is all about Him and not us. He is all we need.

'He makes me to lie down in green pastures; He leads me beside the still waters.'

Verse 3 starts with the words, *'He restores my soul...'*

As I was writing the preceding words, the spirit of the Lord came and ministered to my innermost being. Pause here, tarry awhile and let Him come. I believe He will. Such peace, such beauty, such satisfaction made available to us all by His grace. Thank you Jesus!

It then continues, *'He leads me in the paths of righteousness for His name's sake.'*

We can rely completely on these words because the word of God is truth and in it is written,

'Therefore my beloved, as you have always obeyed not as in my presence only, but now much more in my absence, work out your own salvation with fear and trembling; for it is God who works in you both to will and to do for His good pleasure.' (Philippians 2 :12-13).

In other words it is the Lord who by His leading, enables us to walk in righteousness and although we have a role to play in terms of surrendering and choosing to obey, it is still attained by His grace. In Jeremiah 23:6, this is further confirmed as reference is made to one of His many names which is Jehovah Tsidkenu (The Lord our righteousness).

All of the above verses speak of a time of intimacy, spiritual growth and getting to know the Lord as the one who is powerful, faithful, mighty and true, so that we are then ready, confident and prepared for the trials, tribulations and battles ahead.

Without the preparation, no-one would be able to say,

'Yea though I walk through the valley of the shadow of death, I will fear no evil; for You are with me; Your rod and Your staff they comfort me.' (Psalm 23:4).

As I looked at this verse, I saw the words in a different light which helped me to understand why we must embrace suffering as part of the outworking of our salvation. It is God's plan for our lives that we die to 'self' and live for Him alone. There are also seasons in our lives where God brings us into the working out of this 'death to self'.

They are times of challenge to the attitudes and intents of our hearts. We can feel very low and pressured in these times as God shines His light on parts of our character that need to be purified. We feel like we are in a valley of despair and often it can lead to feelings of hopelessness and desperation as we see how un-christ like we actually are! Believe it or not, this going through *the valley of the shadow of death* although difficult, is a positive time in that it is a period of character moulding.

This is why the writer of the Psalm can say, *'I will fear no evil.'*

We too can say the same thing because God is with us and He is doing this for a reason and that reason is to make us more like Jesus.

Let us read on and consider why the writer then says that the rod and staff are a comfort. How can that be? Again I pondered on these words and the following came to mind.
A rod and a staff can both denote discipline and authority depending on the context. (See Proverbs 13:24 and Exodus 4:17 for the word 'rod' and Psalm 23:4 and Jeremiah 48:17 for 'staff').

When we surrender to God and allow Him to chasten and discipline, when we obey and do what he says, although these things are not pleasant for our flesh and often downright hurt, we should still have comfort in the knowledge that eventually a harvest of righteousness will be forthcoming.

'Now no chastening seems to be joyful for the present, but painful; nevertheless, afterward it yields the peaceable fruit of righteousness to those who have been trained by it.' (Hebrews: 12 v 11).

Dear reader, we are living in an age both inside the church and out, where discipline and obedience to authority are not the "in-words". To God however, and to those who wish to be Overcomers in Him, these words are and their acceptance of them is vital. The next verse of Psalm 23 then says,

'You prepare a table before me in the presence of my enemies; You anoint my head with oil; my cup runs over.'

I felt that the Lord was showing something very significant here.

Consider the state of the society we live in. It is true to say is it not, that there are enemies of Christianity all around? God's commandments are being broken, and what God declares to be good is being attacked. Marriage between a man and a woman is good, discipline, honesty and integrity are good. Purity, modesty, love and faithfulness are good and yet our present society is not mirroring these things as a whole. Should we be surprised? No! The Bible tells us that this will be how things are in the last days.

However, despite knowing this fact, we still have to understand that if we do not keep close to the Lord, the evil will overcome us and our love will grow cold. That is why God has prepared a table for us in the presence of all these enemies and on this table is everything we need to overcome. There is fullness of joy and pleasures at His right hand, there is the blessed assurance that He is with us and there is also the anointing and empowering of the Holy Spirit, so effusive in quantity that it overflows so that others near us will also receive of it. When we get this truth into our hearts we too can say despite the circumstances,

'Surely goodness and mercy shall follow me all the days of my life and I will dwell in the house of the Lord forever.' (See Psalm 23:6)

Chapter Five

We are in a war!

One of the major obstacles we are faced with, which hinders being able to live the life of an Overcomer, is the battle in the mind. This is one of the main areas of focus for the enemy.

Let me ask a question. How do you react when Christians are persecuted for offering to pray with someone who is sick and as a result lose their job?

What are your thoughts when you read the newspaper and are made aware of more and more cases of depravity and abuse against children, the increase in youth suicide and the lack of discipline in schools and at home? How do you react when people make fun of you, misunderstand you, wrongly accuse you or even abuse you for either your faith in the Lord Jesus or for doing His will?

If you are anything like me, and are not careful and constantly mindful of the fact that we are in a huge battle, you can almost feel yourself spiralling down into the depths of being so overwhelmed by all the anti-Christian activity, persecution and sinfulness that you become quite downhearted. This then leads to despondency and, before you know it, total inertia.

Although this is an understandable reaction on a human level, we are supposed to be different, in that, we are to be those who live above the circumstances with the eyes of faith. For this reason, we have been given the Word of God, the Bible: Believers Instructions Before Leaving Earth.

Found within the pages of this book is Jesus Christ himself and, as has already been mentioned, He is everything we need to be made ready, prepared and strengthened for whatever lies ahead. As I travel around meeting groups of Christians, one of my main observations is that often during times of ministering, I discover that the People of God do not know the Bible because they do not spend enough time reading it, feeding and meditating upon what it says, and most importantly, how many of us if we are truly honest really believe what is written in it?

The bible says quite clearly that without knowledge, the people perish and one of the main challenges we face in these days is making a firm decision to devote ourselves to prayer and to the reading of the Word, because it is our sword of attack against the lies of the enemy as he tries to invade our minds and destroy our peace.

We must understand that there is no better weapon than the Word of God and this is because it brings light, life and truth whereas the enemy brings darkness, death and lies. The Spirit of the Lord is urging us to arm ourselves with it before it is too late. If we don't, the door is open for the enemy to come in whenever he chooses and when he does, and we are not armed with the sword, then we will not know how to come against him and defeat his attempts to bring us down.

The parable of the sower, found in Chapter 13 of Matthew's Gospel, illustrates very well the danger of not heeding the instruction, to be rooted in the Word of God. You see, to be rooted in the Word is to be rooted in Him who is the Word: Jesus!

Time to take up arms!

In this story, we read of how a farmer sows seed - which represents the Word of God - to three separate types of people who are represented by the differing types of ground. The second and third examples serve as a poignant warning to us all,

'The seed on the rocky soil represents those who hear the message and immediately receive it with joy. But since they don't have deep roots, they don't last long. They fall away as soon as they have problems or are persecuted for believing God's word.' (Matthew 13:5-6).

The antidote for this potential problem for Christians is found in Colossians 2:6-7,

'And now just as you accepted Christ Jesus as your Lord, you must continue to follow him. Let your roots grow down into him, and let your lives be built on him. Then your faith will grow strong in the truth you were taught, and you will overflow with thankfulness.'

In the third example we read,

'The seed that fell among the thorns represents others who hear God's word but all too quickly the message is crowded out by the worries of this life, the lure for wealth and the desire for other things so that no fruit is produced.' (Matthew 13:70).

A remedy in this instance, is to be found this time in the Gospel of Matthew 6:33,

'But seek first the kingdom of God and His righteousness and all these things shall be added to you.'

This is such a wonderful verse which again points us totally to Christ. In order to be strong, 'Overcoming,' Christians, we have to live surrendered to God's will, and our first focus has to be Him and not the things of the world. If we follow this directive, God promises to supply everything else that we need. We seek the Kingdom by spending time in His presence and allowing the Holy Spirit to reveal it to us through revelation and through the pages of the Bible.

A further cause for major concern is that sadly, speaking from my own experience as a worker in the Kingdom, and just as the writer from the 'Overcomer 1911' wrote in his article, I also find that many are even unaware of what it really means to be called to be part of the army of the Lord - and this is a hundred years down the line.

To think that in 2011 the situation has not improved much since 1911 is pretty disturbing, and not only do many not know how to fight the enemy, as was the case in 1911, they also still do not even realise they are in a battle.

If ever there was a time for the Church of Jesus Christ to understand the necessity of being equipped against evil - and that one of the ways to do this is by immersing oneself in the Word of God - it is NOW. The Lord Jesus has left us with arms for the battles we have to face, but we must take them up.

In Joshua 1:7-8, on the eve of an era of warfare, the Lord spoke to Joshua and said these words which we all do well to heed,

'Only be strong and very courageous, that you may observe to do according to all the law which Moses my servant commanded you, do not turn from it to the right hand or to the left, that you may prosper wherever you go. This book of the Law shall not depart from your mouth, but you shall meditate on it day and night, that you may observe to do according to all that is written in it. For then you will make your way prosperous, and then you will have good success.'

Why? Because as I mentioned earlier, the devil knows his time is running short and he is on full attack against the Church. In my experience as a believer, Christmas time 2010 saw more attacks on Christians in short succession than at any other time I can remember. Just to give you some examples; a Christian was sacked in this nation for refusing to preside over homosexual partnership ceremonies; another Christian was dismissed when she expressed her views on abortion and made the point that not enough attention was given to warning patients of the potential damage emotionally and mentally post-procedure. Churches have been blown up in Iraq and Egypt; 70 Christians arrested and incarcerated in Iran and a Pakistani Government Official assassinated for asking the Muslims to grant clemency to a Christian woman accused of blaspheming the Prophet. The list is enormous and I could go on but I have cited some examples so that we may become aware of the true situation we are facing and take up arms now whilst there is still time.

When Jesus was on earth, He took the time to explain to His disciples that trouble lay ahead but at the same time He encouraged them that they were not to fear. We see this illustrated in the Book of Matthew 10:16-22 where Jesus is warning them that persecutions are coming,

> 'Behold, I send you out as sheep in the midst of wolves. Therefore be wise as serpents and harmless as doves. But beware of men, for they will deliver you up to councils and scourge you in their synagogues. You will be brought before governors and kings for My sake, as a testimony to them and to the Gentiles. But when they deliver you up, do not worry about how or what you should speak. For it will be given to you in that hour what you should speak. For it is not you who speaks, but the spirit of your Father who speaks in you. Now brother will deliver up brother to death and a father his child; and children will rise up against parents and cause them to be put to death. And you will be hated by all for My name's sake. But he who endures to the end will be saved.'

As I have sought the Lord in praise, worship and reading His word, I have felt Him say on more than one occasion that persecutions are coming, and that we are to get prepared and be ready for aggressive spiritual warfare.

I know that 'aggressive' is not a popular word in many Christian circles but we have to remember that when Jesus comes again, it will be as a warrior and not as a babe,

'The Lord will go forth like a warrior, He will arouse His zeal like a man of war. He will utter a shout, yes, He will raise a war cry. He will prevail against His enemies.' (Isaiah 42:13 NAS)

It is the hour where we must accept reality, and the reality is that the call to war has gone forth by God to all of His people. Unfortunately, not everyone is listening or wants to listen. However, to those who have an ear to hear what the Holy Spirit is saying; The Lord wants us to know that ultimate Victory is ours and the Kingdom is ours for the taking, if we keep our eyes on the Commander of the army, seek out His strategy for this war and obey His rules of engagement!

Remember, it is the only war ever to have been waged where the outcome is already assured. Yes, this war will not be easy - it will be long and arduous, and injuries will be sustained along the way; however Christ is the Victor, and with His help we can obtain victory in the battle against the powers of darkness, which at present appear to have gained a winning advantage and seem to be prevailing against us.

Chapter Six

Born to Overcome!

Several years ago I told the Lord that I would do whatever he asked of me and I committed my life totally to Him. Since that time in my walk with God, one of the things He has shown me is the truth about His children being "born to overcome." Below are some examples of this, and the first one occurred just a few days after I had made the decision to follow Christ no matter what.

Overcoming in times of inadequacy

Whilst I was at a meeting, a lady came up to me and said, "The Lord says that you are to get out of the boat. You have been out of the boat, but now you have got back in it, and you are to get back out."

I had no idea what she was talking about and felt rather dejected at her words, nevertheless, the very next day during my prayer-time, I asked the Lord what He meant. What followed was the worst possible response one could have wished for in my case!

God said to start up a "Mothers of Pre-schoolers" group!

He also reminded me that a few days earlier I had said that I would do anything for him.

Now, I need to explain a few points here. Firstly, this was for me my worst possible nightmare. The prospect of working with young children did not enthral me at all. In fact, it is fair to say that I had little patience for them. I much preferred teenagers. I had purposely chosen to become a senior school teacher for this very reason. Secondly, I had no idea whatsoever how to go about doing this. I had no building in mind, no resources and no money to buy them with, and I did not really know what children liked doing by way of leisure pursuits. The thought of cutting, painting and sticking, made me break out in cold sweats!

Admittedly, my youngest was three, but all he ever really played with was a ball (He is now thirteen and gifted by the Lord in sport.) I am hoping you can see the dilemma here but also that you are noticing how at this juncture, all the focus was on my own inabilities and not on the Lord at all.

When I finally said 'yes' in obedience, and began praying for everything I needed, looking unto Him for the ability; looking unto Him for all the numerous resources; the power to fulfil what he had asked of me was supplied.

The Lord brought me a wonderful team, including one who absolutely excelled at doing artwork with the children. The group was used by the Lord to bring his love, salvation and healing to many people, and I was granted such a deep love for small children that now I get told off if I am out with my family because I like to stop and chat with the little ones, and this causes no end of embarrassment! This work is still on-going, affecting lives for good even now, and all glory belongs to God.

Overcoming in times of personal tragedy

Four years ago, my beautiful, courageous mum was suddenly diagnosed with terminal cancer. My mother was my friend, confidante, role-model and loved very deeply by myself and my two brothers. None of us were ready for this, as she was so strong and had always appeared invincible. She had brought the three of us up through our formative years single-handedly, as my parents were divorced when we were in our teens.

Both mum and I are the saved ones from the four of us, (my brothers are still non-believers) but when this news was made public, and I saw the deposits of cancer on pictures that the doctors had taken in her body, I was shaken to the core and ran immediately to the Lord. As for my mum, she never complained, but remained serene as the doctor broke the news.

In fact, apart from an odd occasion or two, she stayed hopeful, faithful and an absolute inspiration to all those around her for the duration of her illness.

As I sought the Lord for strength, He began speaking to me about giants and said that although I was just like David, seemingly insignificant, He said to wage war on this cancer and believe that the Lord of Hosts was behind me. I prayed, I fasted, I wept, I got others to pray and intercede, and despite the fact that after seeing my wonderful mum go through terrible suffering during chemotherapy sessions, we were told it had got worse! After an initial wobble of faith, I refused to give up, hoping that the cancer would go and stood on the word the Lord had given me, keeping my eyes on Him, believing Him and not the circumstances. There were times my faith levels were low but then the Lord would prompt someone to call me or send a card to lift my spirits again.

On December the 29th 2007, whilst in hospital, she died totally unexpectedly, of a heart attack. I had received no fore-warning by the Holy Spirit and had been with her the day before. It was a devastating time, not only for me, but for everyone who knew and loved her. As I stood beside her bed and looked upon her peaceful countenance, I was in shock. I could not grasp the fact that she was no longer with us. Then I felt the Lord say that it was her home-coming moment. He said she had gone into early retirement and I firmly believe it to be true, because no-one in my experience, had worked as hard and as long as my mum had during her life-time. He said He had taken her in this unexpected and quick way because our prayers were holding her earth-bound. The more I pondered on these things, the more convinced I have become that, as excruciatingly painful this situation may be, God, and not the enemy, was in total control and He had the upper hand.

In May 2008, an inquest was held into my mother's death and the Pathologist stated that there was no evidence of cancer in her body! Although I was still filled with great sadness and missing her terribly, it was a momentous occasion for me as I realised how God's ways are so much higher than our ways. As you can see, God did not answer my prayers in the way I would have chosen, but He did heal the cancer, and He showed me that despite what the experts and other people had said, I was in the position of Overcomer and could confidently say,

'Death is swallowed up in victory. Oh death where is your sting? Oh Hades where is your victory? (1 Corinthians 15:54-55)

I can rest in the assurance that my mum is in the loving arms of Jesus and that, given a choice, she would not want to change anything. I miss her terribly and it still hurts to think about her, however, in the midst of the pain, I can still rejoice because God did have the final word and my mum is in Glory!

Three days after her death (she was unable to be buried within the normal time-scale, due to the post-mortem) I flew off to Uganda and ministered to many unsaved souls. God told me to tell the people that the message I was bringing was of the utmost importance, and that He had sent someone to them who had travelled many miles, and whose mother was not even cold in the grave, in the hope that it would firstly prove His love, and secondly, make them realise the importance of heeding the Gospel. It was powerful and God was glorified.

Overcoming in marriage

In the 'natural' I am one of the least qualified people to give advice on this complicated issue. However, our God who is abounding in mercy and love, has taught me a great deal about the keys to a successful marriage and enabled my husband Michael and myself to become trophies of His grace.

We both became Christians within weeks of each other and have been together for nearly twenty years. When one considers that, prior to knowing Jesus, my record for being in a relationship with a man was just five years, there is much to be said about the greatness of God's power, and the undeniable truth of His Word in the area of male-female relationships and marriage.

It is only in recent years that God has begun to bring a deeper revelation on this subject, and I believe that this is no coincidence, but because the heart of God is to restore the intended "right-standing" between the man and the woman. Unless both are reconciled to each other as God intended, the church will be unable to prepare the way for the Second Coming of Christ.

This does not mean that Michael and I now have the

perfect marriage, but from my relationship with the Lord and the willingness to undergo honest assessment of what our roles should be in biblical terms, our marriage has withstood the storms of testing times. Despite us still being 'works in progress', equally, we know upon know, that God's plan for our marriage is that it be a great success, and we are both fully committed in reaching this goal, not only for our own piece of mind but so that He might be glorified.

Ephesians 5:22-33 says this,

> 'Wives, submit to your own husbands as to the Lord. For the husband is head of the wife, as also Christ is head of the church; and He is Saviour of the body. Therefore just as the church is subject to Christ, so let the wives be to their own husbands in everything. Husbands love your wives, just as Christ also loved the church and gave himself for her, that He might sanctify and cleanse her with water with the washing of water by the word, that He might present her to Himself a glorious church, not having spot or wrinkle or any such thing, but that she should be holy and without blemish. So husbands ought to love their own wives as their own bodies; he who loves his wife loves himself. For no one ever hated his own flesh, but nourishes and cherishes it, just as the Lord does the church. For we are members of His body, of his flesh and of His bones. For this reason a man shall leave his father and mother and be joined to his wife and the two shall become one flesh. This is a great mystery, but I speak concerning Christ and the church. Nevertheless let each one of you in particular so love his own wife as himself and let the wife see that she respects her husband.'

From this passage we see two analogies; husbands should be to their wives as Jesus is to the Church. As the church submits to Jesus, wives are to submit to their husbands as to the Lord.

Notice how it also says that Jesus is not only the Head of the church but also its saviour.

As I read these words I realised that this type of headship is one of divine order and not tyrannical leadership. Submission to my husband is not meant to be considered demeaning for me as a woman but to be acknowledged with gratefulness, as it is a vital key to a successful marriage as God intended.

If we pause to consider what Christ has done for us as His people, are we not filled with awe, wonder and thanks that such a tender, loving, wise and patient God should prove his love for us by being our Saviour whilst at the same time being our Head? Husbands are called to emulate Christ in this way by protecting, nurturing and supporting their wives, not 'lording' it over them, but winning them into submission by their love. We are not dealing with cultural anachronisms here, but with a principle that was established back in the Garden of Eden, in Genesis.

If we also take a look at 1 Corinthians 11:3 Paul writes,

'But I want you to know that the head of every man is Christ, the head of woman is man, and the head of Christ is God.'

Moving on to verses 8-9 it says,

'For man is not from woman, but woman from man. Nor was man created for the woman but woman for the man.'

Then in verses 11-12,

'Nevertheless neither is man independent of woman, nor woman independent of man, in the Lord. For as woman came from man, even so man comes through woman; but all things are from God.'

Notice that despite God creating man first and out of Him then brought the woman, He also uses the woman to bring forth man. This inextricable inter-dependence upon each other provides the basis for humility and submission from both parties.

Therefore, *'the biblical perspective is to hold simultaneously the equality and the complimentarity of the sexes.'*[3] If men and

3 The Message of Ephesians by John Stott

women in the church truly understood the depth of these words from the bible, then divorce in the church would be minimal, marriage would undergo a revolution and the world would definitely sit up and take notice.

To overcome in a marriage is not to insist upon our own rights or make demands in any way at all, but to prefer the needs of the other. From my own experience as a wife, neither should my submission to my husband be dependent on how he behaves. It is the responsibility of each individual to keep their side of the requirements before God and allow God to do his work in the other person. On a purely human level, this is virtually impossible, but with God all things are possible, and as we seek God for His grace and empowering, we truly will find that His grace is sufficient.

Queen Vashti has to go!

As you read the following, a story unfolds that teaches women of the potential consequences of not submitting to husbands. I used it when addressing a group of women on this issue, however I am hopeful that men who are reading will also learn from the message.

Queen Vashti is to be found in the book of Esther. In Chapter 1 of this book we read how the King of the Persian Empire was holding a time of feasting for all his people. His wife, Queen Vashti, was also entertaining in the Royal Palace, but only women were allowed to be present.

The story relates how, after seven days of merry-making, the King wished to show the beauty and splendour of his wife to the people and officials and so he commanded that the Queen be summoned into his presence. An important point to remember here is that many influential people will have been present at the Kings banqueting table.

In Esther Chapter 1, commencing verse 12, we read,

'But Queen Vashti refused to come at the King's command brought by his eunuchs; therefore the king was furious and his anger burned within him.'

Continuing from verse 15,

'"What shall we do to Queen Vashti, according to the law, because she did not obey the command of King Ahasuerus brought to her by the eunuchs?"

And Memucan answered before the king and the princes, "Queen Vashti has not only wronged the King, but also all the princes and all the people who are in all the provinces of King Ahasuerus. For the queen's behaviour will become known to all women, so that they will despise their husbands in their eyes, when they report King Ahasuerus commanded Queen Vashti to be brought in before him but she did not come. This very day, the noble ladies of Persia and Media will say to all the King's officials that they have heard of the behaviour of the queen. Thus there will be excessive contempt and wrath. If it pleases the King, let a royal decree go out from him, and let it be recorded in the laws of the Persians and the Medes, so that it will not be altered, that Queen Vashti shall come no more before the King Ahasuerus; and let the King give her royal position to another who is better than she. When the King's decree which he will make is proclaimed throughout all his empire (for it is great), all wives will honour their husbands both great and small."'

In the above account, we find some extremely important lessons on how important it is that Christian women are obedient to the word of the Lord in their marriages. Failing to submit to husbands can have a far reaching, detrimental impact, not only on the relationship of two people, but extend to bringing disrepute on the wider family and even the church as a whole.

Let us firstly look in more depth at the situation Vashti finds herself in. The fact that the King summonsed her to parade in front of the other courtiers was not a wise move on the King's part and Queen Vashti had every right to be annoyed.

However, instead of taking offense and behaving in a haughty manner, she should have realised that not to appear in front of the King was not an option open to her as it would appear disrespectful on her part and thereby send alarm bells ringing throughout the whole kingdom. Her actions would not serve as a good example to the other women who, as her subjects, expected to be led by example.

In the Bible, we see other women who have been forced into uncomfortable situations such as Sarah, when Abraham forced her to pretend to be his sister (see Genesis 20:2) but in contrast to Queen Vashti, Sarah submitted to her husband and God came to the rescue.

The Bible also says that *'Love covers all sins.'* (See Proverbs 10:12) When we fail to realise that a good marriage also accepts the faults and shortcomings of others, we also fail to enter into the bountiful grace and blessing of God who says to each of us,
'Whoever seeks to save his life will lose it, and whoever loses his life for my sake will find it.' (Matthew 16: v 25).

Queen Vashti's behaviour, seen in a spiritual light, was selfish, prideful and fleshy and this sort of behaviour did not contribute to her enjoying a fulfilled marriage. How many times have we allowed friction into our marriages which has had negative repercussions for the family at large just because we were exercising our "right" to be right. As Christians, whether women or men, sometimes for the sake of the greater good, we are expected to sacrifice our own demands and rights so that Jesus is glorified and the world can see that we are different.

Submission should not be considered to be weakness. It takes enormous strength of character and security in who we are, before we are able to enter fully into this and we do well to remember that we do it because first and foremost we love Jesus.

Similarly, although husbands are the Head of the household, they are told that this headship and leading must emanate from a position of love. The authority that they have is not unlimited, but must be in line with God's teaching and principles, otherwise it ceases to exist.

It is very interesting that in the book of Ephesians, although wives are instructed to submit, husbands are not told to exercise their authority at all, but to simply love. God ordained the family order and when this is not adhered to then His purposes and plans are hindered.

If we look at Titus 2:5, we see that wives are called,

'...to be discreet, chaste, home-makers, good, obedient to their own husbands, that the word of God may not be blasphemed.'

However, the fact that a woman does all these things does not mean that she cannot also be brave, strong and have a preaching ministry to the Nations. It does not say anywhere in scripture that a woman may not evangelise, prophesy, heal, deliver or minister if called by God. Consider Deborah the prophetess and Jael that mighty warrior! Also, consider the woman at the well. She was the first female preacher in Jesus' day! and Philip's daughters in the book of Acts who all prophesied.

The fact that women were not permitted to teach in the days of the New Testament was due purely to the culture of the day when women were regarded as lesser beings by society. Jesus did not subscribe to this view at all, and made a point of using women at some very significant moments, such as when he first appeared to Mary Magdelene and told her to go and tell the disciples the "Good News".

We are told quite clearly in scripture that in Christ there is neither male nor female,

'For you are all sons of God through faith in Christ Jesus. For as many of you as were baptised into Christ have put on Christ. There is neither Jew nor Greek, there is neither slave nor free, there is neither male nor female; for you are all one in Christ Jesus.' (Galatians 3:27-28)

The reason I am making this point is because there is a school of thought in the church that is preventing women from reaching their full potential in Christ, in terms of what they are permitted to do.

In the light of biblical evidence; a sincere heart to do only what God wants; to serve the church and the blessing of the Lord on what I have done as a Preacher of the Word for Him; I have to question this stance, and sincerely hope that men reading this book will be blessed and encouraged as much as the women, as they read this chapter. I sincerely believe it to have been downloaded by the Lord. In the book of Revelation we read that it is both the Holy Spirit and the bride who say to the world *'Come!'* to God. (See Revelation 22:17)

Note that, *'The Spirit without the bride does not issue the invitation. The Bride without the Spirit cannot.'*[4] Similarly, a married woman of God will not "go" without her husband's consent but without the wife going and being released into her destiny of God, the husband will not see the Kingdom as God intends. In these last days it is vital that the men in the church release the women, whether they be husbands, pastors or church leaders, and regardless of what the calling of the woman may entail.

4 Footnote on Page 1993 of NKJ Spirit filled Life Bible

A woman shall encompass a man!

One morning whilst in prayer, I came upon a scripture from Jeremiah 31:22,

'How long will you gad about, o you backsliding daughter? For the Lord has created a new thing in the earth - A woman shall encompass a man.'

As I looked at the last section of this verse I prayed for revelation and this is what I believe the Lord showed me.

The word "encompass" means to enclose within a circle; surround; or another meaning is to include entirely or comprehensively. The word "man" comes from the word "geber" which means hero, champion, warrior or mighty man of valour.

The above scripture is therefore saying that this new thing on the earth that the Lord is creating, is a woman that has within her the characteristics which are normally attributable to a man. She will be a hero, a champion and warrior.

This should not come as any surprise because back in the book of Genesis chapter 3, when the woman had been deceived and God was addressing the serpent, He said in verse 15,

'And I will put enmity between you and the woman and between your seed and her Seed; He shall bruise your head and you shall bruise his heel.'

This verse is a promise that one day the Seed of woman would crush the serpent's head and that she herself would play a significant role in bringing Satan down.

Similarly in Proverbs 31, the wife is referred to as being "virtuous". In the Hebrew translation, this word is "chaylil" which means force, strength, able, power, might.

In summary then, it would seem that in the preceding days to the fall of Satan, the woman is chosen to display the characteristics which, in the natural realm, are seen in the

66

man.

The important thing to remember, however, is that despite this shift of role for the woman in the spiritual battle for the Kingdom, it is not an opportunity for the wife to usurp the authority of her husband nor adopt a haughty superior attitude. The divine order of God still stands.

As I meditated on the above it struck me that God is requiring great humility on both His male and female children. Yes, the female is going to be used mightily in the last days and will be the on the front line of the spiritual battle, but this does not mean that she thereby turns into some feministic-macho!

No, on the contrary, she is still to respect and submit to her husband. In fact because of the authority as Head of the Household, it is his job to release his wife and encourage her to step into her God-assigned role because unless he releases her she cannot move forward. It is also his job to be her "saviour" in that he must guide and support her in it, if this is her calling. They are to be mutually dependent on each other, under the Headship of Christ.

This is so contrary to male behaviour in the world that I believe it has to be God. Only a secure, strong, spirit-filled man with a heart for God could allow this apparent role-reversal to take place, and I thank God that my husband has recognised the call of God to be such on my life, and he has completely released me. Not only that, he supports me in every possible way and for that I am so thankful to the Lord.

J.H. Yoder wrote, *'Equality of worth is not identity of role.'*

It is my firm belief that for the church to overcome in the coming days, both Men and Women have to work together in their assigned roles under God with humble and sacrificial hearts.

Overcoming in times of financial uncertainty

I felt compelled to include testimony about this issue because I know that for me personally, the thought of not having financial security has caused me no end of misery in the past. It would not be right to say that I am now completely free of this fear, although God has always been faithful, and so has my wonderful husband who supports me admirably.

This problem stems from when I was young and often heard my mum saying that she was worried in case there was not enough money to pay all the bills. This impacted my subconscience then, and has since been an area of contention in my life.

However, Jesus Christ shed His blood for my peace, so I am not content to remain here but have made a decision to become free and will continue praying for the ability to do so.

One thing is certain, and that is that the Lord in His goodness has brought me a long way from where I started! This journey to freedom is not an easy one, as it involves times of choosing to trust God and to have faith, rather than allowing fear to take hold.

On occasion I do feel rather afraid, but it is the refusal to succumb to fear that matters in God's eyes. When He sees that our hearts are just longing to be able to trust Him, He shows up with enough grace for us to move forward and enter into greater freedom and faith, as opposed to being stunted in our growth and paralysed by fear.

As I pondered about what I should share, I felt to tell you what some of my journey has been like so here it is; an amazing testimony to the greatness and effectiveness of being in covenant with God!

In the year 2008, there was a crash in the financial markets and my husband, whose business is in the financial sector, suffered a major downturn. As a consequence of this, our financial situation became so critical that, just before Christmas, my weekly standing order for the house-keeping and personal living expenses had to be stopped, as the bank was not prepared to help us in the crisis.

It is also worth mentioning that 2008 or 5769, "Samekh Tet" according to the Hebraic Calendar which starts in September, means, "A year of God's goodness in the midst of suffering." I am certainly a living witness to this fact as you will see!

I want to share with you an entry I wrote regarding what was going on in December 2008;

> '*I have just had the boiler and Aga serviced with a bill of over a hundred pounds. Then 2 days later, the boiler breaks down which means no hot water or heating. Michael is working very hard but we realise that we have to put the house up for sale as it is too expensive to run. Before we can do this we have the problem of a hall which needs decorating as there is no wallpaper on the walls. In addition, the drains keep overflowing outside, there is something wrong with the electrics as the lights keep tripping and then the woodburner breaks! To make matters worse, my brother calls me with a bill for £300 which is my contribution for my mum's grave-stone and then, just as we feel it cannot get any worse, the oil light indicates the need for more fuel and the last bill had been £600.*'

In addition, although I did not put this in my diary, I had standing orders to meet upon which the livelihood of certain people in Africa depended, and finally, I was supposed to be going on a prayer assignment to Tunisia, but the money I had saved had to be spent on house-keeping costs.

On the evening that Michael rang to tell me that the bank

was refusing to help us, I was on the verge of a break-down and felt like giving up as it had been such a hard year and both Michael and I were physically and spiritually exhausted. However, I remembered a scripture that I had read that day from Hebrews 3:14,

'For we have become partakers of Christ, if we hold the beginning of our confidence steadfast to the end.'

So I got down on my knees in the kitchen and prayed very fervently, reminding God that because of my obedience to Him, I was in covenant and it was therefore His job to provide as He was my Jehovah Jireh.

I then began a three day fast, and managed by God's grace to ignore the turmoil inside, and speak positively into the situation by speaking aloud the word of God and thanking Him in advance of seeing anything happen for what He was going to do for me.

These are some of the scriptures I declared.

'There is no want to those who fear Him. The young lions lack and suffer hunger; but those who seek the Lord shall not lack any good thing,' Psalm 34:9-10

'He who has pity on the poor lends to the Lord, and He will pay back what he has given.' Proverbs 19:17

'But seek first the kingdom and His righteousness, and all these things shall be added to you.' Matthew 6:33,

The power of declaration and a positive confession is often under-estimated in the church, but as I began declaring the truth of God's word over my situation, my attitude changed and so did the circumstances.

Not only did God sort out every problem I had, he supplied over and above my needs. I had money sent through the post, groceries delivered to my door, someone felt the Lord was telling them to pay for my flight to Tunisia. The oil bill cost half of what we had anticipated and we received a gift for the full amount. God was absolutely astounding!

At the beginning of this chapter, I explained that both Michael and I were exhausted and I mentioned this to a friend of mine who suggested that we pray for a free holiday. I began to pray and then met someone who had just returned from the Lake-District.

Apparently the place they had visited offered respite to worn out Christians! I sent them an e-mail and explained our situation and they gave us a long-weekend for absolutely free!

Since this time, God has been faithful in the area of my finances on every level even though I am called to work full-time for Him and therefore do not go out to work as such. Obviously my situation does not apply to every Christian, and we need to be clear on where the Lord wants us regarding our work. I know that I am in the right place and I know that God will supply my every need.

Last year I went to North Korea - the most expensive trip imaginable for me - and the money came in. This year, the Lord said I was to launch this book in Uganda and a few weeks ago I received a substantial love-gift which will pay for the whole trip.

Principles for financial security!

I now want to explain the principles that have helped me personally to reach a greater level of faith and assurance in the Lord with regards to the area of financial provision. In sharing them with you, it is my hope they may be of help to those who like me have suffered from a fear of financial insecurity.

Proverbs 3:9 says,

'Honour the Lord with your possessions, and with the first fruits of all your increase; so that your barns will be filled with plenty, and your vats will overflow with new wine.'

Principle One

Submitting to God and walking in covenantal relationship with Him in all areas of life. If I am obedient to God, I can expect blessing and not curse, life and not death, abundance and not lack. In regard to this issue, I have submitted the whole area of my finances to God. In other words, whenever He says give, I give, even though it makes me nervous on occasion! By following this principle I have found that the giving opens the way to receiving. In fact, if I need some money for God's purposes, I will ask the Lord where I am to give some away.

I once received a picture whilst in prayer. It was of a large grain storage tower and it had a small door at the bottom from where the grain could be extracted upon demand. Every time the grain was needed and taken away, new reserves of grain were added from the top so that the grain store was never empty. I felt the Lord say that the tower represented our finances, and as often as we give to the needs of others as directed by Him, the provision would never run out. I am a living testimony to that fact.

Principle Two

Whenever anything extra comes as a gift from the Lord, like for example a love-gift for speaking at a meeting, I always give Him a tenth as an offering of my thanks.

Principle Three

Give the Lord the best! One time I had made some jam which had taken a great deal of time and effort and the Lord asked me to give two jars away. I first of all picked up the two smallest jars but felt so challenged and humbled that I put them back and gave of the bigger ones. I saw immediately the selfishness and covetousness in my heart and had to repent.

When we pause to think the price that Jesus paid for us on the cross and how God gave His only son, we have to reciprocate in whatever way we can, no matter how small because He is worth it.

Principle Four
Pray to receive the gift of giving. Human nature is selfish and covetous but through petition and a willingness to trust, we can allow the Holy Spirit to make us into joyful givers. There are so many needs in the world that God wants to fulfil. If we wish to be vessels of giving, God has to trust us that when He gives, the resources will be used for His glory. We need to pray that God will make us such people.

To conclude, I invite those of you who feel God is speaking to you through this chapter, to read the scripture on the next page and to "test" God at His word. It will be scary at first but as my story has shown, God will not disappoint as you step out in faith.

'Do not rob God' from Malachi 3:8-10

'Will a man rob God? Yet you have robbed me!
But you say, "in what way have we robbed you?"
In tithes and offerings.
You are cursed with a curse,
For you have robbed me,
Even this whole nation.
Bring all the tithes into the storehouse,
That there may be food in My house,
"Try Me now in this,"
Says the Lord of Hosts,
"If I will not open for you
The windows of Heaven
And pour out for you such blessing
That there will not be room
Enough to receive it!"'

Chapter Seven

The journey

Over the past few years, I have done numerous exploits for the Lord, despite being a normal "run of the mill" housewife and mother in the eyes of the world. I have been sent on various evangelistic missions and prayer assignments world-wide, and on several occasions I have been directed by God to preach spontaneously in the middle of city-centres, pray for the sick in the street, give complete strangers words of Knowledge and, when directed by the Holy Spirit, randomly approach people with the challenge of the Gospel.

The fact that I have done these things is not because of who I am, but more a case of who He is. Of course the one who created us and knits us together knows the course He has charted for our lives and therefore places within us personalities and characters that make us prepared for the call. But the plan God has for each and every one of His children is to go beyond the "natural" into the "supernatural" realm. It does not matter what the call and giftings are, what concerns God is our obedience to Him in the fulfilment of them, for His glory and to be a witness for God to this world.

If only we could take hold of this truth and not allow the whisperings of the enemy to hold us back from our destiny. It is time to believe God and to believe His word and gain encouragement from it. It is time to understand that the feelings of inadequacy, insufficiency and inability are pre-requisites for being usable by God. God humbles the proud but exalts the lowly!

However, true humility before God is not that we feel so unqualified that we never get out of the pew and do anything for the Kingdom - oh no! That is not being humble, that is walking in unbelief. True humility is the realisation that of ourselves we can do nothing, but in Him we can do all things, and refusing to allow doubts and fears to hold us back.

Moses' story

Let us consider the man Moses. Most of us know the story of how he was rescued as a Hebrew baby and adopted by Pharaoh's daughter. Then after spending his formative years in the palace, he became a lowly shepherd because he mingled into the affairs of others and ended up murdering someone and had to flee. His qualifications for service started out okay but have now taken a turn for the worse, and we could be forgiven for assuming that God would never use a person with these credentials under his belt.

And this was not all, as the story of Moses unfolds, more character weaknesses are exposed which we will look at and examine in the scriptures starting with Exodus Chapter 3. We see that in verse 1, Moses is to be found at the 'back of the desert' in other words, in the "back of beyond" but as we read on, we see that in this seemingly forsaken wilderness where nothing extraordinary ever happens, where his hopes, dreams and aspirations have all but disappeared and died, it says he came to Horeb, the mountain of the Lord! It was here in the most unlikely of places that he was positioned for purpose!

Perhaps at this moment you too find yourself in the "back of beyond" in your own situation. Like Moses, you also have virtually lost all hope of ever being "strong" in the faith and able to be used by God. You may have health issues, financial problems, relationship breakdown, disillusionment, problems with children, and so on.

Oh yes, you had a vision once and you have received words over your life but you have endured so many set-backs and gone through so many trials that, to be honest, you are beginning to wonder whether these words ever had any truth in them at all.

Under no circumstances do I wish to undermine the suffering and pain that we often go through as God's children, but we do have to ask ourselves the questions: How are we reacting at this time? Who are we trusting? Who are we believing? Who is in ultimate control of our lives?

The Bible tells us that we will have to suffer for the gospel but as we endure and keep our hearts right, the Lord Jesus promises to be with us. Isaiah 63:9 reads,

'In all their affliction He was afflicted and the Angel of His presence saved them.'

Also the good news is that when you are in this place, just like Moses was in this story, you too are positioned for purpose!

Let us continue ...

In verse 2, the Angel of the Lord appeared to Moses in a flame of fire from the midst of a bush. Now these bushes are very common in the desert, and also very unattractive. God could have chosen something of beauty to appear to Moses in, but he didn't, and one interpretation for this is that for the increase of the glory of God to be seen, the flesh has to die so that the presence of the Lord within us is what remains visible.

This flame was the "Shekinah", the glory of God's presence which transformed everything and everyone it touched. In other words, God visited Moses through something of no significance of itself and makes it special and holy. This is a wonderful illustration of how God wants to be seen in us.

Going back to the story, we read in verse 10 how God commissions Moses,

'Come now therefore, and I will send you to Pharaoh that you may bring my people, the children of Israel out of Egypt.'

However, in verse 11, Moses says,

'Who am I that I should go to Pharaoh, and that I should bring the children of Israel out of Egypt.'

Instead of accepting the call and trusting God to work through him, Moses reveals his fear and lack of knowledge regarding his identity as a child of God. Even when God tells him He will certainly be with him, Moses is still not convinced, and what becomes evident in verse 13 is that not only does Moses not know who he is, but he also does not know the one he is supposed to be representing. He showed a lack of intimacy as he asks God what name he should give when asked by the Israelites who had sent him.

How unlike another shepherd of the bible David, who in total contrast knew his God when commissioned. We can still take heart however because at the end of his life (see Deuteronomy 34:10) Moses is described as a man whom the Lord knew face to face.

As we read on, we see how God does not dismiss Moses as a lost cause, but perseveres with him despite further displays of unbelief, more fear and more feelings of inadequacy and finally, in what is such a show of love, grace and mercy, the Lord allows Moses to enlist the help of his brother Aaron who will act as Moses' spokesman before the people of Israel and Pharaoh.

Those of us familiar with the life-story of this seemingly inadequate man will know that the Lord went on to use Moses in extra-ordinary ways that he most probably could never have imagined in his wildest dreams.

Similarly, God has done the same in the lives of many of His Disciples including myself (not to the same degree in my case, I hasten to add, but that does not mean that he can't!)

My story

I was conceived out of wed-lock and brought up in a typical working-class Catholic family; the eldest of three and the only girl. The fact that I was a girl did not bode well for me as my father had wished for a boy, and throughout my whole life, until encountering my heavenly daddy, I never knew the delight, satisfaction and security of a Father's love. Hence my perception of both men and a 'Father' was completely warped and the pain of rejection was buried very deep in my heart.

At the age of eleven, I went to Grammar school and initially I felt very proud at having gained a place and worked hard mixing with the 'nice' girls. Unfortunately however, at about the age of thirteen, missing a bus one night changed the course of my life to my detriment.

Before I go on to explain what happened that night, I have to tell you that when I left the Grammar school, in the eyes of the staff, I was a complete "write-off" a "no-hoper". Despite having passed the eleven plus, due to my rebellious behaviour, I left school with hardly any qualifications. I felt totally lacking in self-esteem and self-worth and considered myself a failure even though I hid these feelings behind a veneer of vociferous self-confidence.

To go back to the story about missing the bus... I had arranged to meet some friends and we were going to a youth club but the bus arrived late and they had left. I felt afraid and abandoned on that bus-station but then I saw a group of girls from my year at school who were known to be quite "wild". They called me over and invited me to go out with them and I said 'yes' when I should have thanked them but declined their offer.

I do not have any desire to exalt the work of the enemy, so suffice it to say that this wrong choice led to a season of dissipation and unhappiness which was to cast a shadow over my life for the next twenty years, until I met with Jesus.

I experienced total breakdown in the relationship with my Father, as my parents got divorced when I was fourteen, and then went on to experience two broken marriages and the agony of divorce. The second divorce was so traumatic that it left me with depression and anxiety and, to make matters worse, two of my children were involved.

This was my complete and utter breaking point, but shortly after this divorce was finalised, I then came to faith and it was also at this time that God brought me the husband of His choosing which is Michael, with whom I have a third child called Thomas.

I am not saying that when we know the Lord there are no troubles or shadows in our lives but the difference is that before I knew Jesus, in times such as these, there was no-one I could really turn to that could bring the depth of healing that was needed to my heart. And as I did not know of Him, apart from as being some untouchable religious icon, I often felt totally alone and lost.

Since knowing Jesus however, despite the fact that there have been times of great suffering, I know that there is a place I can go to for comfort and restoration that no human being can ever offer me, and that is in the safety of His Presence.

Of course during the time of separation from God, He was

still gracious to me and there were periods of great joy. I had a tremendous mum who stood by me and loved me through all my mistakes, even though she herself was not a believer at this stage.

All my life I had had such a desire to travel and see the world, so it came as no surprise to my mother when, at the age of barely seventeen, I caught a bus to Barcelona and never returned home from then on, apart from brief visits. I travelled from Spain to Portugal, and then onto Germany, where I studied hard to learn the language which I managed with a degree of success. I got a job as an air-stewardess and then fulfilled the dream of my childhood which had always been to travel the globe!

Despite these positives, the baggage of the past was still being towed around with me and I had several unsuccessful relationships which I walked out of as easily as I had walked into.

Now as a Christian, I realise that the inability to commit to anyone stemmed from the fact that I was afraid of rejection, but at that time I seemed totally oblivious to the hurt and damage I was causing to others. After being an air-stewardess in Germany, I married for the first time and moved back to London where I got a job in the fashion business. Our circle of friends at that time were mainly graduates, and this highlighted my feelings of inadequacy greatly.

The marriage only lasted a couple of years, and to cut a long story short, a few years down the line I was married to someone else, and living up North near my mum with two children under the age of two and yet another disastrous relationship on my hands.

My second husband was a highly intelligent Lawyer who, as far as I was concerned, represented all I longed for. I was in awe of him and now see that I actually idolised him somewhat.

He had the qualifications and the public standing I longed for but he too was hurting and wounded, and despite the gift of two adorable children whom God has blessed enormously, our marriage was a complete failure, but neither of us had the ability to fix it.

My husband did not have much faith in my academic prowess and this caused me no end of distress, so when a German examiner extended the opportunity to do a degree at university, I jumped at the chance even though I had two children still in nappies and was by now involved in a very traumatic divorce.

This degree was to be a huge learning curve for me - a lesson that God was going to teach me even though I was still a couple of years away from knowing Him. I came through with a First Class Honours degree in European Business Administration and Languages, and even won the Student of the Year Award. I had never won anything, apart from maybe a school raffle and a beauty contest at my Dad's work's party at the age of 9! and strange though it may seem, the first person I thanked, upon reading my result, was God, and then my mum.

In those few euphoric moments I thought I had "arrived" so to speak, but within a few days, the excitement of those moments had faded and as I reflect on those days, I have realised that God's idea of success is absolutely nothing in comparison to the world's view. In fact, although I trained to be German teacher and was considered to be a good graduate and a good teacher with excellent promotional prospects, the Lord said that I was never going to be a 'high flyer' as a teacher and, after just four years in the profession, He called me out to be totally focussed on Him.

I was now a House-wife and mother! You tell that to people at some dinner-parties and it causes uncomfortable silences and embarrassed coughs, as people dismiss you in a flash as being someone of no consequence. Once again I was being shown very clearly, that the ways of God are so much higher than our ways, and in order to be Overcomers, when it comes to the standards of this world, we have to allow Him to place us in situations which cause the pride of man to die. He has certainly done that with me and I have to confess that I still find it hard when people look down on me because I seemingly do not contribute financially to the household, or have to say that I am a house-wife.

My prayer is that I will grow to be so secure in Him and realise more fully my identity in Him, which in truth is all that is needed, that the views and opinions of men will be of no concern but only what God thinks will matter.

'...He has no form or comeliness, and when we see Him, there is no beauty that we should desire Him. He is despised and rejected by men A Man of sorrows and acquainted with grief. And we hid as it were, our faces from Him; He was despised, and we did not esteem Him.' (Isaiah 53:2-3)

Perhaps the most challenging of these lessons came when I was called to train as a Local Preacher in the Methodist Church. It was such a hard journey for me, with pain and persecution on the way, and I could not wait to qualify and get into the pulpit with God's undiluted Word!

However, shortly before my final results came through, whilst walking out in the countryside, I distinctly heard God's still small voice say to me,

"Linda, are you prepared to lay this down for me. You do not need a title to have a preaching ministry and I'm asking you to lay this down."

I had metaphorically speaking, sweat blood and tears for over two years, and gone through so much that these were the last words I wanted to hear but sure enough, it was God who spoke to me, and although I passed all the assignments and had a super report for my assessed service, I never received the title of being a Local Preacher.

The scripture God gave me was John 12:24,

'Unless a grain of wheat falls to the ground and dies it remains alone, but if it dies it produces much grain.'

In summary, I came into the Kingdom a completely wounded and unsuitable candidate for anything of any substance. There was shame, rejection and condemnation on me, and I really did not feel worthy to be loved. But our God is a redeemer, a healer, a restorer, a lifter of heads and a great encourager who loves His children unconditionally and never tires of telling them so, if only they will take the time and make the effort to listen.

It is from this position of security in His love that again and again the Lord has brought forth fruit in my own personal life, which is so very encouraging when one considers where I came from.

However, in order to step out and bring forth the fruit, fear, intimidation, feelings of inadequacy and even hostility on occasion had to be overcome. This would not have been possible had I not trusted God and I am, therefore, totally convinced that if we are to embrace the call on our lives and complete the race of faith, we need to be secure in His love, understand the truth and faithfulness of who He is and believe that the promises of the Lord are Yes and Amen in Christ Jesus. (See 2 Corinthians 1:20). I can say with overwhelming thankfulness in my heart and to the glory of my saviour that the person I was, no longer exists.

In Christ I have found total acceptance and total love and for that reason, no matter what or who may come against me, I can truly say I believe that when I became born again, I was born to do exploits for the Lord, and I was born to overcome every obstacle that would try and prevent me from doing this!

This is His message to everyone who knows Him as Lord and Saviour!

No-one has been more surprised than I have at how God can do mighty things through ordinary people who are willing to press into God, make Him their number one priority, be available to Him when He calls, and love Him enough to be prepared to take up their cross and follow Him.

It fills me with such hope as I read the life-stories of some of our heroes of faith from the past and present, but these heroes are too few and far between when one considers the number of citizens in the Kingdom. This is the hour when God requires all of His children to rise up into their callings and destinies and realise that we all have a responsibility and a part to play in the ushering in of God's Kingdom.

It is time to believe God at His Word and overcome all the doubts and fears by taking our eyes off of ourselves and fixing them on Jesus who says to us all,

> 'My grace is sufficient for you, for my power is made perfect in weakness. Therefore I will boast all the more gladly about my weaknesses so that Christ's power may rest on me. That is why for Christ's sake, I delight in weaknesses, in insults, in hardships, in persecutions, in difficulties. For when I am weak then I am strong.'

(2 Corinthians 12:9-10)

About the Author

Linda Robinson is a disciple of the Lord Jesus who fervently believes that with God NOTHING IS IMPOSSIBLE and that when a person is born-again, they ARE BORN TO OVERCOME!

She lives in the Lake District with husband, Michael and is a house-wife, home-maker and mother to three children: Christian, Lauren and Thomas.

Linda is convinced that this is the season for the True Church to arise against the enemies of God and bring in the end-time harvest for His Kingdom; in His righteousness, strength, might and power.

This is Linda's first book and she can be contacted on born2overcome1@hotmail.co.uk

Bibliography

1. The Overcomer. Volume III. 1911
Edited by Mrs Penn-Lewis

2. The Bible Speaks Today: The Message of Ephesians
by John Stott (Inter-Varsity Press)

3. Master Plan by Jane Hansen Hoyt
(Aglow International Publications)

Acknowledgements

Unless otherwise indicated, Scripture quotations are taken from:
THE HOLY BIBLE, SPIRIT FILLED LIFE BIBLE,
NEW KING JAMES VERSION.
Copyright: 1980, 1982, 1991 by Thomas Nelson, Inc. All rights reserved.

The following abbreviations have been used to indicate where other Bible Versions are quoted:
NLT - NEW LIVING TRANSLATION
Scripture quotations marked NLT are taken from the Holy Bible, New Living Translation copyright 1996, 2004.
Used by permission of Tyndale House Publishers, Inc., Carol Stream, Illinois 60188. All rights reserved.

NIV - Scripture quotations are taken from the HOLY BIBLE, NEW INTERNATIONAL VERSION.
Copyright 1973, 19778, 1984 by International Bible Society.
Used by permission of Hodder and Stoughton.
All rights reserved. 'NIV' is a registered trademark of International Bible Society. UK trademark number 1448790.

Lightning Source UK Ltd.
Milton Keynes UK

178270UK00001B/2/P